10670337

THE SASH HE NEVER WORE ...
TWENTY FIVE YEARS ON

By Derek Dougan

Attack

The Sash He Never Wore

On The Spot

The Footballer

Football As A Profession

The Doog

How Not To Run Football

Matches Of The Day

The sash
he never wore ...
twenty five years on

DEREK DOUGAN

LAGAN BOOKS
&
ALL SEASONS PUBLISHING

Copyright © Derek Dougan 1972 1974 & 1977

Introduction © Percy Young 1972

All rights reserved

The moral right of the author has been asserted

First published by Allison & Busby Ltd

This edition published 1997 by
Lagan Books and All Seasons Publishing
Unit A, 17, Valley Business Centre,
67 Church Road, Newtownabbey, Co. Antrim,
N. Ireland BT36 7LS

ISBN 0 85031 070 9

No part of this book may be reproduced or transmitted in any
form or by any means without written permission from the
publisher, except by a reviewer who wishes to quote brief
passages in connection with a review written for insertion in a
newspaper, magazine or broadcast.

Printed and bound in Great Britain by
Butler & Tanner Ltd, Frome and London

*THIS BOOK IS DEDICATED TO THE MEMORY OF MY MA
AND DA. JOSIE AND JACKIE WHO WERE SIMPLY THE BEST.
AND TO MAISIE AND JOE "THE DUKE" HENNESSEY DITTO!*

CONTENTS

Preface/xi
Introduction by PERCY YOUNG/xv

I HOME
1   "What the Irish were made for"/19
2   "One big dream?"/29
3   "A great deal in common"/41
4   "The stand gutted, the grass growing wild"/53
5   "An apprentice had to start somewhere"/65
6   "Desperate to get out"/77

II AWAY
7   "A very clean place"/101
8   "Some hard truths"/109
9   "Too many have lost the art of wandering"/123
10   "A man's game"/137
11   "International"/145
12   "Charity begins at home"/155
13   "None but an Ulsterman can fairly criticise
        Ulster"/167

Epilogue/161

BACK HOME
14   "The football game—the final score"/165
15   "Hatred ... where does it come from?"/181
16   "Man's Inhumanity to Man"/197
17   "Josie and Jackie"/205

Solo Sure I'm an Ulster Orangeman. From Erin's Isle I came
To see my Glasgow Brethren, all of honour and of fame,
And to tell them of my forefathers who fought in days
of yore;
All on the twelfth day of July in the sash me father wore.

Chorus It's ould but it's beautiful. It's the best you ever seen.
Been worn for more nor ninety years in that little
Isle of Green.
From my Orange and Purple Forefather it descended with
galore.
It's a terror to them paypish boys—the sash me father
wore.

Solo So here I am in Glasgow Town youse boys and girls to see,
And I hope that in good Orange style you all will welcome
me,
A true blue blade that's just arrived from that dear
Ulster shore,
All on the twelfth day of July in the sash me father wore.

Chorus It's ould but it's beautiful *etc.*

Solo And when I'm going to leave yeeze all, "Goodluck" till
youse I'll say,
And as I cross the raging sea my orange flute I'll play,
Returning to my native town, to ould Belfast once more,
To be welcomed back by Orangemen in the sash me
father wore.

Chorus It's ould but it's beautiful *etc.*

*Traditional Irish song but not to be
sung by all Irishmen; only those
who wear the sash my father never
wore.*

    D.D.

LIST OF ILLUSTRATIONS

1*a* Derek's mother
 b His mother and father on their wedding day
 c As a baby
 d At eleven months, with his older sister Pearl

2*a* Sandy Dougan, Derek's grandfather
 b With his father and pigeon trophies
 c As a boy
 d With father, brothers and sisters

3*a* Derek outside his grandfather's pigeon loft
 b East Belfast street ready for "The Twelfth"
 c The Dougan house in Avon street, now boarded up (*photograph by Stanley Matchett*)

4*a* The Belfast dockyards
 b At Grosvenor Park, with Jackie Curry
 c In Italy, with the Northern Ireland Youth Team, 1955

5*a* Distillery Youth Team, 1957, in Belfast
 b Distillery F.C., 1956, at Grosvenor Park (with three Catholics and seven Protestants)

6*a* In a Portsmouth jersey
 b Blackburn players looking at the Wembley turf before the Cup Final of 1960 (*by courtesy of Evening Telegraph Ltd, Blackburn*)

7*a* Meeting Vic Crowe, the club captain, on joining the Villa in 1961 (*by courtesy of Albert Wilkes*)
 b Failing to score in the Fifth Round Cup match, Villa v Charlton, in 1962

8*a* A training session at Leicester in 1966 (*by courtesy of Birmingham Post and Mail*)
 b Peterborough v Bournemouth, 1963; a heading

9*a* Scoring for Leicester against West Ham, with Jim Standen in goal, in May 1966 (*by courtesy of Peter Robinson*)

  b Injured during Leicester v Sheffield Wednesday match, 1966

10*a* Things one shouldn't have done—at Highbury, 1969

  b Communicating with the Wolves crowd after a goal

11*a* Elation shared with Jim McCalliog after a Wolves goal against West Bromwich Albion, November 1969 (*by courtesy of Monte Fresco*)

  b One that didn't go in (*by courtesy of Reveille Newspapers*)

12 The Wolves battle against Karl Zeiss Jena F.C. in the U.E.F.A. Cup, 1971-2: above, in the Ernst Abbe Stadium, Jena (*by courtesy of Fotosports International*); Below, at Molineux

13*a* With the Northern Ireland Amateur International team before the game against Wales at Ebbw Vale in 1957

  b Captain of Northern Ireland before the match against Cyprus, in the Nations Cup, Windsor Park, 1971 (*by courtesy of Jack Casement*)

14*a* A charity walk, for Mental Health Research, in 1971

  b Working on the book, with Percy Young (*by courtesy of Wolverhampton Express and Star*)

  c At Radio Birmingham, 1971

PREFACE

When I wrote "The Sash He Never Wore" a quarter of a
century ago in my naivety and innocence I never realised
it would invoke the darkest of sentiments and deepest of
fears from the quagmire of Northern Ireland's bigotry that
lies just below the surface of our community life.

Much has happened in the years since I put those words
together. Northern Ireland has seen all of the terrible
agony and despair of twenty five years of what we have
come to call simply, and in an underestimating way, "The
Troubles".

My late father, Jack, was asked, Why did Derek call the
book that name?"

The question brought out the fiercest side of my father
in response, the side that was loyal to his first born son.

Depending upon who was asking the question the answer
could take on different forms. . . .

Had the question been asked out of genuine enquiry,
intellectual pursuit if you like, the answer would be easy
and helpful and polite.

But when the questioner was there for malice and for
stirring up the quicksands of Ulster's sectarian desert, Jack
would with ease and pride and loyalty and determination,
respond in the tough language of this riveter from the
shipyard of Harland and Wolff. If he knew what you were
up to and if in his view it was no good, then Jack wouldn't
beat about the bush. You would get his answer.

And apart from anything else everyone in and around Dee street, Medway street and, Avon street where I was brought up, knew that my father was never an Orangeman and neither was his son.

But those with their own ideas would always think it and then say it.... Derek Dougan can say what he wants but he isn't here, he isn't in the firing line, so he can have the luxury of writing a book with such a title. It was a cutting and deeply hurtful allegation.

That, as they say in Ulster, was then but no one can level that criticism at me now for I have been back in Ireland for more than a decade. I have been living in Belfast for the past five years and have seen the suffering of the Ulster people at first hand. I have experienced it.

When I was in England, writing the first book (The Sash He Never Wore) and keeping closely in touch with home I was always naturally concerned at times of the worst atrocities. When bombs went off and the killings took place I would worry and be immediately on the phone to my dad and members of the family.

"Had the bomb been close to home or work?"

"Had anyone we knew or loved been hurt?"

The agony was all the more because I was distant and in no way able to contribute to the safety, the security and well being of those I loved and cared for.

The relief in hearing, and I love this phrase, "no problems, all's well" was always immense.

But when replacing the telephone receiver pangs of guilt started rushing through me. Although my family and everyone I knew were safe, the guilt set steadfastly in ... it had been someone else's mother, father, son, daughter, wife or husband. A quarter of a century ago ... a long time past when those calls were made but life never changes. Whilst sitting at my keyboard writing these words the thoughts of my relief and my guilt came flooding back.

Scotland, Dunblane, sixteen people dead ... a slaughter

of the innocent by a deranged gunman ... that's what the news was telling me and the lady said, and she was an Ulster woman, "When I saw and heard that my own child was safe I was greatly relieved but then came the guilt for at that moment of relief I knew that my good fortune was someone else's tragedy."

Tragedy ... Tragedy, it's a word that shudders the human spirit and in the Northern Ireland context it is tragedy not for a quarter of a century (such an easy phrase it trips off the tongue), not at all, but now almost thirty years. Thirty years of a tragedy which all of us believed would never last, would go away, would leave us alone. ... But no, the tragedy is still with us.

The politics of the late nineties are the politics of the old. Politics and politicians ought to have done more for the people they represent.

Old means lack of youth, old means close to death, old means fear and an inability to change. Think about it, our politicians today are the politicians of almost thirty years ago and today when the talk comes round to progress the word that is feared most and most times absent is the word trust.

On the one side the argument and the slogan came, "Fifty years of Unionist misrule" and then men began to sit down together for people and for progress. But progress was continually blocked. Those who had considered themselves badly done by in the past were now not for taking chances; there would be no generosity, there would be, No Trust.... No Surrender.... No Talking.... No Going Back to old ways.... No Talking...just in case we agree ... and, all the while, the people who didn't live in the big house on the hill, the people who queued for giro and benefit at the Newtownards road post office and at the post offices on the Falls, they and only they were the ongoing victims of the terribleness of the happenings of the night.

It's a long way of saying it but it's my way of saying it, the good and fair minded people of Ulster have not got the politicians they deserve. They deserve better and in a world that sees conflict resolution occurring more and more in the most difficult of theatres and scenarios, the simple Ulster dilemma of being unable to trust is the funeral dirge that follows the deaths of the masses.

Twenty five years ago I wrote:

"Government is a contrivance of human wisdom to provide for human wants. Men and women have a right that these wants should be provided for by this wisdom."

Belfast
26th June 1996

INTRODUCTION

It may reasonably be said that Derek Dougan is one of the great footballers of our age. He is one of the few who will leave his mark indelibly on the game. This will be seen to have been done in two ways: first, by the exposition of rare technical skills; second, by the pressure of his influence on the administration and by the application of a keen analytical sense to general problems and difficulties. The link between the two functions—of player and administrator—is that faculty which, for want of a better word, we term the imagination.

The imaginative quality of Derek's play—certainly in its maturity—is what gives to it a particular richness. There have been a few great players whom I have known who have been able to bring the world to a standstill by their genius in expressing a philosophy of life through the medium of a leather ball on a few square yards of grass. These players, like actors, perform their assigned roles in such a way that they provoke awareness of some of the issues that cast shadows over the general conscience.

Football is a very ancient craft, joining together ritual and art, and in the final issue being a sublimation of those aggressive instincts that both create and destroy. In Renaissance times the mystical union between art and football was solemnised under neo-Platonic sponsorship, in Venice by the same Count Bardi who (as near as makes no odds) invented Italian opera. The particular quality of Italian *calcio* of the seventeenth century—that is, its aesthetic virtue—to some extent at least is realised by Derek Dougan, whose present control of a match is assured by swiftness in analysis of situation and by economy and delicacy in the consequent physical action.

All the world that knows how to appreciate football knows that in Dougan there is one of the artists of the game. For my part I would go further: he is an artist. Beyond that—or within that—he is an Irishman.

In the professional sense, art is my concern—I would like to think all art, even though competence may be limited to a small sector. At the beginning of a career in music I found myself in Belfast, where I was required to instruct intending teachers for the schools of Northern Ireland. It should be said that the students and the schools with which my duties lay were Protestant. I remember that in those days—in the mid-thirties—armoured cars were sometimes to be seen in the streets of Belfast, that the general tenor of life was not quite even, and that it was a brave man who made observations on the state either of religion or politics.

I recently turned up a letter, from a Belfast colleague of pre-war days. It was written to me after I had left the Province, and among other things included reference to a Northern Irish General Election. The year was 1938.

> Great excitement prevails here over the Election. One of the candidates, midst loud cheers and beating of big drums, stressed his resemblance to the late Lord Carson and also pointed out that his birthday, the Election date and the birthday of the late Lord Carson were on the same day!

The historian needs no footnote to see a connection between then and now.

It happens that while in Belfast I had opportunities to meet persons of great distinction in that city (who were both hospitable and approachable), and also to establish a lasting academic relationship with Dublin. In other ways too I was absorbed into Irish life and able intimately to become acquainted with some part of its glories and its tragedies.

One advantage of my first appointment (though I did not perhaps see it as such at the time) was that it took me into the less than fashionable parts of Belfast. In Derek Dougan's descriptions of the scenes which are the back-cloth to his own life I find a particular kind of truth—the artist's truth. That is to say, Avon Street, Dee Street, the Springfield Road, and so on, are brought vividly before one through the acute perceptivity of the artist. I do not need to say that Derek's skills in the other art, of football, centre on an acute perceptivity—the same perceptivity, in fact.

It was inevitable that at some time or other I should meet Derek Dougan. This meeting having been effected (we signal jointly our gratitude to Phil Morgan) it was equally inevitable that in reviewing our experiences and interests we should discover a whole wide area worthy of closer investigation.

There is, of course, no reason why this should not be so, but there is an opinion frequently held that footballers and musicians can have nothing in common. This is a horrible heresy. It is indeed the heresy that created the situation of disaster which aroused in us a joint concern and a feeling of some responsibility.

When communities of people find nothing in common distrust grows into hatred, and the barricades go up. When individuals shelter behind barricades and feed on their own thoughts and prejudices they not only miss half of what makes life worth living, but also develop an exclusivity that denigrates the next man.

There is another heresy that is commonly aired. Politicians everywhere are the first to enunciate it as a cornerstone of faith, and there are many in many callings who are glad to hide behind it. This or that, the article goes, must be left to the politicians. Rather more feebly the man (or woman) of jelly faces a great moral issue with the inspiring statement that " . . . it has nothing to do with sport/art/literature/ business . . . it is politics." The Irish problem is what happens when politicians are taken at their word. It is fair to say that the Irish problem is exclusively the creation of the politicians, and that it is only those who in the professional way are not politicians who will be able to solve it. One says "the Irish problem", but it is not: to the Irish it is surely "the English problem". There are many blood-stained pages of history to show it. The extent of English ignorance in respect of Irish history is illimitable and any reduction of this ignorance is a step towards the achievement of peace in Ireland. And since peace is indivisible it is a step towards peace.

At the same time the realisation of a reasonable way of life in Ireland makes demands on its own people, whether from north or south, whether at home or abroad. This book stemmed from a twofold sense of obligation. One who has been brought up in Ireland has his own obligation, especially to those left at home. One who at one time was engaged in Irish education also has his obligation. At various times the two of us discussed the general theme of obligation in certain circumstances, and the relation of professional to civic responsibility. Neither of us could find a line at which at least a recognition of responsibility could stop.

The footballer is a citizen. Derek Dougan's acknowledgement of this fact and his refusal to walk away from the distortions and inequalities that disfigure human existence are at the heart of this book. I have before me the transcript of a television programme in which Derek was involved in discussion of the state of his native Province. At one point he said:

> Well, I don't wish to opt out and I won't opt out, but sometimes I think about the situation—I'm an Irishman and also I'm an Ulsterman. And this is the dilemma that faces me.

Thoughts shaped into spoken words—sometimes by way

of question and answer, sometimes by way of dialectic, sometimes through spontaneous eruption—were transmitted to paper via dictaphone. There followed periods of discussion, of amplification, and of revision. In so far as I have been an active participant in this book it has been to use such professional expertise in the field of letters as I possess to keep a main channel navigable. It is not only Derek Dougan's ideas that are here, but also his words. Often one stands back from them and wishes that one could be as explicit. I must confess that in this expression of an Irishman's creed there is much that is deeply moving.

There was a passage in a book about prejudice and distrust between racial groups in the southern States of the U.S.A. that we read one day. The words lie somewhere near the roots of *The sash he never wore*:

> I had not tried to give her answers. I had tried only to give her understanding of the difficulties of her elders— of all of us who have failed so miserably in the culturing of children. Knowing that bitterness is a poor bent key to use to unlock the future, I wanted her to begin her search for answers with sympathy for those who had not found them. I knew it would be hard enough for her who so passionately loved her ideals and a family that did not share them. *

Percy Young
Wolverhampton
January 1972

* Lillian Smith, *Killers of the Dream*, W.W. Norton & Company, Inc., New York, 1949/61, pp. 74-5

I
HOME

1

"What the Irish were made for"

I was born in Belfast, which is in Ulster, and Ulster is Northern Ireland. That is, the part of Ulster sliced off from Ireland some fifty years ago is Northern Ireland. I thought that the only things that were important took place on the east side of Belfast where I lived for my first eighteen years. It was through my involvement with football that I came to realise that there were things going on in the world outside the domain marked off for me by the Newtownards Road, Avon Street, the River Lagan, and the Hollywood Arches.

I was fourteen or fifteen when I was first made aware of the "Free State" as another country. I was one of a party of fifteen from the Boys' Clubs of Belfast, representing Cregagh, selected to go down to Dublin to play against the pick of the Boys' Clubs there. We caught a train at the Great Northern Station to take us abroad and into the "Free State".

We were oblivious to everything outside the purpose of our trip and to pass the time we indulged in the ritual game of cards. My mind kept going back a few weeks earlier, to when I had been ill and in bed with the 'flu. There had been a final trial to decide the team for Dublin, and I had been so desperate to take part that I had persuaded my father to let me get out of my sick-bed to play. After thinking about it a bit, he told the people who organised the trial that I wasn't at all well and should not play. He was informed that it would not make any difference; that so far as I was concerned it was only a formality. I would, they promised, be in the side anyway. However, in the end, I did play in the trial, and it turned out to be not "just a formality". It took place in awful conditions. It was raining very hard and there was a strong wind blowing (to this day I have not got used to playing in windy conditions). I was also weak from the 'flu, so I did not play very well. I did not make the side and, although I was in the party, I had only been chosen as a reserve. That was one of the great disappointments of my life. I would have travelled to the world's end for a game of football, which was all I was interested in from the age of ten.

I went on the trip hoping that someone would cry off. So I set out from Avon Street with my boots. At least these were the best turned out of any. They were well cleaned as always—thanks to my Da who looked after them—and had a new pair of laces in them. As it happened, I did not take part in the game in Dublin (which resulted in a defeat for us—two-one or three-one). But the trip itself was exciting enough. And in a vague way I now knew that there was a "Free State" and a border.

Not that we ever talked about these things much, if at all. Really I cannot recall the subject of the division of Ireland ever being seriously mentioned down Avon Street. One thing I knew for sure: I never looked on the other part of Ireland as another country. I did know, however, that the people there—the vast majority anyway—were Catholics.

When I now come to think of it, I must have known all the time that the "Free State" existed, even though I was not to meet anyone from there until I was fourteen or fifteen. It was like this. A great many people from the north used to go down to the "Free State" on special day trips. My mother went quite frequently, and she always came back laden with butter, cheese, eggs, and other foodstuffs, because south of the border one could buy them for half the price that had to be paid up north. Towns I remember her visiting in the south were Dundalk and Monaghan. As a matter of fact, I can never recall that she went to Dublin; there were excursions there, too, but I suppose they cost too much for my mother.

Before each of these trips my mother would scrimp and save for a month or two. She travelled by bus—never by train. What worried her about going down south wasn't crossing the border—which wasn't then the fearsome thing it is now—but that after she had been into the "Free State", and had spent her money and bought her goods, she and the rest of the party had to stop at the Customs control to be searched. Sometimes whole parties had been stripped of their goods, it was said.

Looking back, it doesn't seem important whether the two States (Eire and Northern Ireland) had any love for each other or not, because each did serve some useful purpose for the other. Northerners made coach trips to the "Free State", where they spent their money and boosted the economy. At the same time they were able to buy goods there that were a lot cheaper than in the north.

When we think of the border between north and south we Irish think of towns like Newry, Dundalk, Monaghan, Drogheda, Armagh, Londonderry, and Donegal. Most English people who have never been to Ireland would have no idea that these places are all near the border. I know people from both sides of the border, of course, but it is only since 1969 so far as most people are concerned that these little places have come into world prominence.

Before all this I played football in many border towns and I made acquaintances in them. One of my colleagues at Aston Villa was Peter McParland, who played thirty-five times at outside-left for Northern Ireland. Peter came from Newry, which is just in the north, but started his football career with Dundalk in the League of Eire. A later colleague in the Northern Ireland team was Pat Jennings who also came from Newry, where he learned his football. Both of these friends are Catholics and among the nicest people I have had the good fortune to know; full of humour, of kindness, and tolerance.

If you look at the map of Ireland you will see how ludicrous it is that we have two States—and that when you talk about the South you may very well be talking about parts of it that are north of the North. If you go, for example, from Eniskillen to Letterkenny you go from North to South, but you travel from south to north. How silly can you get? But what is silly in this case is tragic.

When I went to Dublin with the Boys' Club party I cannot remember that the train stopped, or that we were inspected, or asked where we were going. We certainly were not asked why we were going into the "Free State", in the way that people are asked why they want to go from eastern into western, or western into eastern Europe. We got into the train at the Great Northern in Great Victoria Street and two hours later arrived at, I think, Connolly Street Station in Dublin. We played the game against boys of the same age and I cannot remember any sort of hostility, or that any of the boys didn't want to play against their opposite numbers. I enjoyed the day out and so did the rest of the party.

In 1957 I went to Portsmouth. It was at first like being a foreigner. Most people assumed I came from Belfast *or* Dublin (these were the only towns they knew of over there), but nobody ever seemed very sure which. Of course, the citizens of Portsmouth couldn't tell the difference between a northern and a southern Irish accent. But this never stopped anyone from teasing me on account of mine. Within a few weeks I found out that very few indeed of the people I came across had ever been anywhere near Ireland. I had once had a big day when I went to Dublin. For those people in Portsmouth their big day was a trip to London. If I had turned things round the other way I could have looked on them as less than first-class citizens—because they had never been to *my* country.

For a thousand years the Irish have been treated like second-class citizens. Sometimes not even as good as that. Later in life I have found out that what happened in Ireland, because of her nearness to a big, powerful, often dictatorial neighbour, happened to a lot of other countries. I have been to Poland, to Czechoslovakia, and to Albania, with the Northern Ireland football team. The first time I went to a poor country in eastern Europe I wondered why the people were as they were. It wasn't until long afterwards that I learned how the Poles, the Czechs, and the Albanians—as well as many other people—had once been dominated by the Austrian Empire.

In Belfast we were always taught that the way to heaven was through hard work, and if you really put your back into it you could get some of the good things of life on your journey. I never thought of asking why, if this was so, all the people on Avon Street who did work hard didn't look much better off than those who didn't work at all—because there wasn't any work.

When I first came to England I did not come across any Irishmen (outside the employment of the Portsmouth Football Club) in any important job in—for example—industry, politics, or entertainment. All the Irishmen in England seemed either to work on the roads and the building sites or on farms. There were some to be found in licensed premises—on both sides of the bar—of course. Most priests of the Roman Catholic Church are Irish by birth or by descent. In every hospital there are Irish nurses. But the Irish were not fit, it seems, to be employed in professions other than these. I resented the attitude that was general in much of England, that these jobs were what the Irish were made for.

I was very young and inexperienced then, and I did not reckon—as I might now—that England owed a very big debt to Ireland simply in economic terms. (What would you do in England if you had not a mass of people across the water ready to come and work for you, sometimes through plain

hunger, always because of under-development at home?)
And I was not cheered up—as to some extent I now am—by
the marvellous contribution made to the life of Britain by
the best brains of Ireland.

After Belfast, I found it very different to live in a town,
like Portsmouth, where there are many ways of life in the
same community, and where you can really see how other
people live. In Belfast, this was never encouraged.

The English, however, have strange views about Ireland
and I firmly believe that the attitudes they hold have been
passed down from previous generations. The connection
between England and Ireland from early days was too often
like that of a stern teacher and an unruly, or an unhappy,
pupil who never knows for what he is being punished. Once
upon a time I knew a lot about that.

Moving to Blackburn from Portsmouth I found that the
Lancashire people differed from those in Hampshire. The
people in Portsmouth used to tease me about the supposed
habits of the Irish, in Blackburn they didn't do this—presumably because of the influx of Irish into Lancashire where
once there was work for them in the factories.

In Birmingham, where I lived for a time, I had quite
another kind of experience of attitudes to Ireland and the
Irish. I think there are only two places in England with more
Irish than Birmingham. One is London, the other is
Liverpool. The "Brummies", it seems, think that the
Irishman works on a building site from Monday to Friday
and then spends all Saturday and Sunday drinking Guinness.
After the pubs close, though, friendship is thought to go
away and every "Paddy" is supposed to find another and the
two of them then fight the bit out for the next two hours or
so—unless the police break it up. Ten years ago there were
parts of Birmingham where this might have appeared to be
the truth. Every fight was outside a pub. If you were driving
past, or riding in a bus, you were sure to hear someone say,
"Ah—there they go. The Irish are at it again!" In these areas

the situation has changed. It has changed through the immigration of coloured people. It is no longer the Irish who suffer the insults of the prejudiced. It is the new immigrants.

Since the end of the war many different nationalities have come into Britain and people with roots in many far-off places have become British subjects. As a result of all this the Irish have been up-graded. They are as a group no longer at the bottom of the immigrant pile. But I don't think that they are all that far away from the lowest rung of the ladder. They say truthfully that the Irish have long memories. I wouldn't be all that certain that the English are as good as they think they are at forgetting old prejudices.

It is odd. Since I have established myself in the sporting world I am allowed some privileges.

I have been very lucky in being a professional footballer. It has been a sort of passport for me, and through playing football fairly well I have come to be accepted in many places which otherwise might not have been so welcoming. Football opens many doors for me and takes me across many frontiers. Sometimes I think of all the Irish who don't have this kind of opportunity. I am immensely grateful, of course, but I reflect with some irony on the situation. I am removed from the class distinction argument. I also have the impression that I am no longer regarded as a real Irishman. I am the footballer, the one who brought out that book, the one who is always on television, the Chairman of the Professional Footballers' Association. As a sportsman I—like others—am given special priority and, as I say, am apart from the class business. I don't think this is very fair to the great majority of people.

One of the reasons that I became involved deeply in my own profession, and now help in the running of the P.F.A., is that I had become conscious of the profession having been kept under, and inhibited, for the three quarters of a century professional football has been recognised. It is only in the last four or five years that the profession as such has been treated with rather more respect. Respect for the profession, by the way, is a different thing from enthusiasm for this or that player. It has only been achieved by us having had opportunities to negotiate with the top administrators of the Football Association and the Football League. My Committee are fortunate that they can now put problems concerning the welfare of players to these important bodies with a chance of finding solutions or easing difficulties.

After spending many years fighting a complex coming from the "second-class citizen" tag that used to be tied round the neck of every Irishman whether from north or south, I have come to one conclusion at least: that when one person can be accepted by society it is a shame that obstacles are put in the way of some sections of the community—just because they have a different colour, just because they have a different creed, just because they are from another country.

When I look across the water I see how the little man in the street in Belfast—and it doesn't matter whether it is a Catholic or a Prostestant street—never has the opportunity to put forward the real problems that upset his life. Many problems, it seem, can never be dealt with; others cannot be dealt with quickly enough. This is the tale of woe. The crux is that the people at the top are, or at least for a very long time have been, ignorant of what life is like at the bottom. If ever they become aware of the situation they are unwilling to do anything about it. And at the root of all this is the cancer of prejudice.

Edmund Burke possibly was the greatest Irishman of all time—if he wasn't, he has marvellous qualifications for the title. He was born in the southern part of Ireland. His father was a Protestant and his mother a Catholic. He was sent to a Protestant school in northern Ireland and finished his education in the Protestant University of Dublin. He married a Catholic. Burke went to England, where the power lay, and fought tooth and nail for all the principles he thought worth while. He was the champion of slaves, of Catholics, of the American Indians, and, most of all, of the Irish he had left behind and whose needs and miseries he knew best. He was a member of the British Parliament, and he did what his conscience told him was right. He spoke out for free trade for the Irish and for Catholic emancipation. Because he did he was disowned by the people of Bristol who had elected him.

We could do with a statesman like Burke right at this point in time. Most of all we could do with one in Ireland. Of whom at this time can it be said that he dedicates himself to "great, just, and honourable causes"? That is what someone wrote about Edmund Burke. He himself had this to say in one of his speeches, and it can be addressed to Ireland at this time:

> Government is a contrivance of human wisdom to provide for human *wants*. Men have a right that these wants should be provided for by this wisdom.

2

"One big dream?"

My mother and father used to tell me that the Dougans originated from the country—from a little place called Comber, six miles outside Belfast, going towards Dundonald, in County Down. It was inevitable in those days that the countryfolk came to the big city to seek their fortune. My grandfather came possibly to seek his, or at least to get regular work. I was told that in those days Belfast's major industries were Harland and Wolff, the rope-works, Gallahers and the linen industry. Harland and Wolff is a famous shipyard; Gallahers is a tobacco company. My grandfather chose to work in Harland and Wolff. He was a boilermaker and he finished up as a foreman.

All the generations after my grandfather—my father and his brothers and even down to me—eventually finished up in Harland and Wolff. That's how it was in those days and I think the same stands now.

My grandfather's name was Alexander but from my early life I always heard people call him Sandy—if they were lucky enough to call him by his first name. And it was as Sandy Dougan that he was always revered. He seemed to be a man of enormous height, round about the six foot mark, I think, and typical of the grandfathers in my day. They ruled the roost.

My grandfather lived next door to us, and if I was in trouble with my mother or my father he never had to say anything to me. He only had to look at me and I would have run a mile. He was an interesting man, a hard worker and an ex-footballer, who wouldn't leave Northern Ireland to go and play in Scotland because he could not take his racing pigeons with him.

For the record my grandfather played football for Stormont. This was a good junior side in a part of Belfast that has become better known because of its Parliament building. The half-back line of Stormont was at its most reliable when Sandy Dougan was at right-half, Willie Stitt at centre, and Billy Ritchie at left-half. Sandy played well enough to be offered a place with Hearts, in Edinburgh. But his pigeons were more important. I am told that Sandy got interested in pigeons when he lived in Comber. The story goes that he used to walk from Belfast to Comber to get his fancy pigeons, which were called Tipplers. (He had a lot of good fortune with them. He had thirteen Penzance Cup winners and he won this Cup outright. This wasn't all. He also won outright the Old Bird, Young Bird, Cross Channel and Average Cups outright. The day he won the Penzance Cup outright he had the only bird that was able to finish; it was a very bad day, with a strong north-east wind.) My father inherited this love for pigeons and he too became something of a fancier.

My grandfather had big bushy eyebrows and a middle parting in his hair, which was very fashionable in those days, particularly among centre-forwards, like Lawton and Dean. He was a man who always wore a stiff collar, always was immaculately dressed, always had a bowler hat! The bowler hat was part of his Masonic outfit, for he belonged to this Order.

I was very young when my grandfather died, but I can remember two or three things clearly. I had become interested in football just before his death and he was very critical of me. I was a budding centre-half in those days and I was rather left-footed. As he watched me practise, or play about, he continually criticised me for using my left foot too much.

I remember every Saturday night, too, because my mother used to tell me what the argument was that I heard from my bedroom when I was supposed to be asleep. It was always about the "Glens" or the "Blues"—Glentoran and Linfield Football Clubs, that is. It was equally bad whether the wee Glens beat the Blues, or Blues beat the wee Glens. My father's elder sister Sadie and my Uncle Tommy McNeelly were very, very staunch Glentoran supporters and, of course, since my grandfather had nearly played for Linfield his loyalty remained. Apparently my grandfather was known as being very cantankerous and even if the wee Glens beat Linfield decisively, three or four nil, he would give no credit to them.

It may as well be said here that there was football throughout the family. My great-grandfather, John Dougan (after whom my father was named), was part-time grounds-man at the Oval—the old Oval, that is—until he got the sack. This was because of prejudice. My great-grandfather, so I'm told, worshipped Johnny Darling, a Blues' player who won a number of international caps, and spoke of him as though "he was God Himself". The Glens' directors were jealous because they considered that Darling should have been a Glens' player since he belonged to East Belfast. The directors once told my great-grandfather to put Johnny Darling out of the ground. Naturally he refused to do this. So he was put out of his job instead.

As well as two sisters, my grandfather had five brothers. Four of them were footballers. Dick played for Old Ormiston, a club on the other side of Oval. Later on he emigrated and worked in the Bethnal Street Works in New Jersey, in the United States, where he died. Great-uncle Johnny emigrated too. No great footballer, he also settled in New Jersey where he became a head foreman. The best tales were those that were told about my grandfather's brothers Bob and Bill. Bob was a ball artist. He won a number of

junior caps with Linfield for whom he played inside-left. Bill
was a "slasher". One Christmas Day, the story goes, the time
that people talk about "brotherly love", Bill hit Bob during a
Linfield-Glentoran match. Bill felt he was being made to
look a fool by his brother. For giving way to his feelings he
got four weeks' suspension. It may be that for a player to be
sent off for hitting his brother in this way is unique. There
were, of course, many other stories told about footballing
Dougans of long ago.

I remember my grandmother Dougan much better that
my grandfather and I really knew her much better. She was a
very homely type and hardly ever went out of the house,
except to go to town, or to market. And she was enormously
generous. I was her blue-eyed boy, and could go to her when
I had any sort of trouble. In those days I was picture-crazy; I
used to go to the pictures almost every day of the week. She
would lend me the money to go and I paid her back when I
had my pocket money.

There was one thing I used to tease her about a lot in those
days. Like an awful lot of women where we lived, she took
snuff. When she took a pinch we both sneezed together. Now
and again she would give me a little to sniff, and of course I
would sneeze half a dozen times.

My grandmother was a great cook and I remember how
she used to make all the home-made things like potato bread,
soda bread, and intricate dishes like the good old Belfast
"fry". This one never gets in England and I always look
forward to it when I go back to Belfast. There was a dish that
my mother also used to make—I think we used to have it
Tuesday or Thursday in the summer—called "Champ". It is
difficult to describe this to the English even though it
consisted only of mashed potatoes and—as we used to call
them—scallions (in England these are called, I believe, spring
onions). Once a week my grandmother used to put all the
cream of the milk into a big butter-milk bottle and for one or
two hours I would have to shake this—it seemed for ever and

ever—until I could see the cream eventually turning into butter. My grandmother used to have the stove going and a hot plate on it for the fresh potato bread or soda bread. These waited for the fresh butter and if you have never tasted this then you haven't tasted anything! We always had this every Friday, and a wonderful treat it was. Our feeding, by the way, followed routine and the same dishes turned up on the days of the week set apart for them. Away back everything always looked the same, and everybody thought that that was the proper way of things: no change.

When I look back on my childhood and to the environment that I came out of, and I see the present-day situation, I believe that it was one great big dream. I can't really visualise myself as having been born there, or coming from Northern Ireland.

My Granny Dougan was a sort of protectress. When I was at school at Mersey Street, the headmaster was a very rough horrifying type of man. He was brutal, and I never forgot the day when he caned me—he was not blessed with good eye-sight and aiming at my hand he hit my wrist (there was a current of brutality in the education that I knew). I went home looking for some sort of sympathy but unfortunately I didn't get any because my mother told me that I must have done something wrong to be punished. I went to my grandmother (of course), who looked at my wrist, which was by that time very swollen, then put on her coat and went round and gave the headmaster the rough edge of her tongue. This was the kind of her relationship with me. She felt an awful lot and she was so warm that I probably spent more time in her house than in my own, because we lived next door to each other. I always found it a warm place and loved going to see my Granny Dougan.

Great-aunt Nelly—one of Grandfather Dougan's sisters—had a son who became a minister in the outlying parts of Belfast, but I can't remember at all that my grandfather himself was religious, and think that it was my grandmother who looked after the religious side of family life. That was the way of it then; all grandmothers in our neighbourhood looked after religious matters. And certainly Granny Dougan was the best church-goer on the Dougan side of our family.

Although born Church of Ireland we never went to the St. Patrick's Church which was along the Newtownards road, but always seemed to go either to a little Methodist or Presbyterian hall, where I got the best part of my religious education, or to a little Baptist hall. My grandmother used to go round three or four evenings a week and these little halls were practically full of church-going people seven nights a week. I went quite often because after the service, or the meeting, as it was called, was over we all had a cup of tea and a couple of biscuits. As I am a great tea-drinker this was a sort of incentive to go round with her. There was a real, homely, party atmosphere. I expect it all sounds very old-fashioned. And so in a sense it was. They were very old-fashioned people and set in their ways. But I liked being with them and no one had to blackmail me into going to the "meeting". Besides, in those days I was genuinely interested in religion.

My Granny Dougan was indeed a kindly soul, but there were occasions when I would hear her using four-letter words. Since those days I have heard other people using the same words. I may have used them myself. But immediately Lizzie Dougan caught on what she had said she would turn up to her maker (as she called him always) and apologise three times. "God forgive me, God forgive me, God forgive me!" And she promised that she would never say the bad words again. She found it hard to keep up with her promise, needless to say.

As we lived next door to the Dougan grandparents, naturally one saw more of them than of my grandmother and grandfather on my mother's side.

I first came across my Kitchen grandparents during the war years when we were evacuated from Belfast to Bangor.

This, of course, impressed me a great deal, for Bangor was on the County Down side of the Lough and one could see the boats steaming by. When the war was over we came back to the city. My grandfather, however, used to travel backwards and forwards from Bangor to Belfast to work every day until they returned to live in Thistle Street. It was a sort of Sunday outing for me to go and see my mother's mother and father, and I didn't get to know my Grandfather Kitchen as well as probably I should have done. He was in the same mould as my Grandad Dougan, and he too worked in the shipyard, where he was a fitter. He was a disciplinarian, a very strong man in personality if not in stature. He lived with my Aunt Belle and my Uncle Frankie for many years until he died. My Granny Kitchen was similar to my Granny Dougan. She was, I recollect, rather warm and affectionate. That side of the family was not quite so addicted to football. Still, my grandmother had two brothers who played, surprisingly, for Belfast Celtic. They were Jimmy and Alfie Wishart, both inside-forwards.

The world has changed so much since the last war that it is difficult to think how little there once was to do, and how few were the chances of boy and girl meeting. About the first meeting of my father and mother one may presume three or four possibilities. They could have met at a dance. They could have met in the picture house. They could have gone walking together. There is the chance that my father was invited home by one of my uncles who had got to know him in the shipyard, and that it was in the Kitchens' house that my father first met my mother. In fact when I checked up I discovered that they met in the "New Un"—the New Princess Picture Hall (we called cinemas still by this old-fashioned name).

Belfast is marvellously situated, and one of the things I clearly remember about my childhood was that every Saturday or Sunday we used to go for long walks from the east side of the city to Victoria Park and even beyond it. If you were fortunate enough either to have a motor-car or a bicycle you went down to Bangor or Newtownards to enjoy the sea-side and the marvellous scenery. It took about twenty-five or at most thirty minutes by bike, and even today, when I go home, I find that the situation hasn't changed all that much, except that there is not the same walking in Victoria Park since a dual carriage-way was built. When I look back on my childhood in Belfast, which I now know better than I did when I was a boy, I sometimes wish that I had had the chance to get to know west and north Belfast, and to walk up the river Lagan and up the Ormeau Road, which leads to great beauty spots. The fact is that it is only in the last ten or twelve years, since I came over to England, that such landmarks as the Cave Hill have really appealed to me. This is a wonderful sight and within ten minutes of the centre of Belfast. I often recall that tremendous hill with the clouds rolling down over it, bringing rain—endless rain it sometimes seemed—to Belfast.

Rain reminds me of a game we used to play in Avon Street. In those days the drainage wasn't all that good and when there were heavy showers inevitably the street filled with water quite quickly. We used to see how far we could jump across the water at its widest point in the street. On one particular day I was going for the biggest jump across the road and I took an enormous run. I got across the water all right and cleared it, but unfortunately I had Wellingtons on and slid along the road until I crashed into a set of iron railing which every house then seemed to have. I had a huge cut on my forehead. As soon as I got home my mother took me up to the City or Royal Hospital (I forget which). It so happened that my father had gone off to Dublin—or somewhere in the "Free State" anyway to have a weekend with the boys. He didn't know anything about my accident. It must have been Easter, because he brought me back a big Easter egg, and I remember my Grandfather Dougan shouting at my father for going away for a weekend.

My first days at school were in Bangor, and when I went to
that school I believe I was one of the youngest ever to go
there. I was only three years of age.

When we came back to the City I went to Belvoir School
and I remember that I was very good at two things as a five-or
six-year-old "infant". It was not reading, but writing and
spelling, and we used to have a marvellous competition even
at that age. The kids got stars for the best written work and
the most correct spellings and my book, or "jotter", was
always full of stars, which I knew would please my mother
and father.

After Belvoir I went to Mersey Street School from about
the age of eight or nine till I was thirteen years old. There are
some brilliant schools in Belfast and in Ulster—such as
Campbell College, Methodist College (or "Methody" as it
was known), and the Academical Institution ("Inst"). There
were many more high-class schools which I couldn't have
gone to because of the economic situation of my family.

I went to Mersey Street School because it was the nearest
to my home. The school was not far from Dee Street. Avon
Street, where we lived at number thirty-one, was at the
bottom of Dee Street. Away along the Newtownards Road
was Thistle Street, where my grandparents—the Kitchen
ones—lived, and that ran away from Susan Street where in
fact I had been born. East Belfast was a place of its own and
Mersey Street School was an important part of it.

The two things I remember most from Mersey Street were
starting playing football, and the headmaster who was called
Mr. Johnson. He was an exaggerated example of my
grandfather, and literally ruled the school by terror. When
we saw him on the prowl, when he came into our class (or
into any class), we all immediately took an interest in what
we were doing. It wasn't worth getting into trouble with the
teachers because of the canings. If you did not have it on the
hands you had it on the pants, and as my pants were not
too thick in those days, I preferred it on the hand—until the

time Mr. Johnson missed and hit my wrist.

Another teacher I remember was Mr. Mawhinney, because he took an interest in my football as well as my work. There was also a lovely Welshman, Mr. Jones, who was the sports-master. At the time Mersey Street had a great footballing tradition and one of its great rivals was Temple-more Avenue. Football was a matter of great prestige, and the masters used to try to find as many good and promising players as possible.

It was just by accident that Mr. Mawhinney once saw me running round the playground after lunch. I never stayed at school to have lunch because there was my elder sister and my younger sister to think about. My mother couldn't really keep me there and not the other two, so we all went home every day, and every day we had a fry and I still never got tired of it. I was about nine when Mr. Mawhinney saw me running round the yard after lunch, and he felt I could expend my speed and energy on a football field.

It's funny to think that Mr. Mawhinney must be bordering on fifty, or even over fifty now, for I remember him as plainly today as he was twenty-five years ago. He was rather dashing and had thick hair. His dress was rather unusual for our part of Belfast, but typical of a schoolteacher of those days. It was the sort of sports-jacket with leather patches on the elbows. Really one could tell a schoolmaster by looking at his clothes.

Right from the start my interest academically was in spelling and mathematics, called "sums", and especially in algebra. I quite liked history, but geography I didn't take much notice of. I have never been good with my hands, so woodwork, which they took a great interest in at Mersey Street, was not for me, but I was very keen on music, or rather singing. Unfortunately we only had about half an hour a week and I always wished I could have had more. I thought I was not a soprano, but a version of Mario Lanza, who was my hero, and of course I wanted to sing all his type of songs. Unfortunately the teacher didn't know any of those or she couldn't play them. After learning the scale—do, re, mi—off by heart, which was the be-all and end-all of the music lessons, I rehearsed and sang all the Mario Lanza songs and I knew them backwards.

Just as I was leaving school they introduced gardening and I got very enthusiastic. There was a patch of ground in the middle of the school where they grew potatoes and all sorts of vegetables and that caught my interest because I already helped quite a lot in our back garden in Avon Street.

After school we would normally play football from about four o'clock until tea-time, at five or six o'clock, and then go, almost every night, to the pictures, which were changed every Monday and Thursday. If the film was good enough we would even go to cinemas in east Belfast miles and miles away. It didn't matter how far we went, because we went in numbers, and always protected each other. I said 'almost every night', but we couldn't go and see pictures on Sundays because it was against the law and I believe it is still the case. Ulster still holds fast to Puritan ideas—which is part of its character.

The pictures which captured my imagination in those days were those of Hop-a-long Cassidy, Jesse James, Errol Flynn as Robin Hood, John Wayne's films, "Superman" and so on. They used to have unending heroics to whet your appetite, and you would go back next week because you were afraid to miss anything.

If you were fortunate you had a radio in the house, but for many people in those days there seemed nothing else to do but go to the pictures. Nothing reminds me more of how it was an escape than those fantastic "Tarzan " pictures. In Belfast now it seems there is no escape: the call of the wild is a grim, horrifying, bad dream that is real.

3

"A great deal in common"

My father went to Mersey Street School, so it was inevitable that after leaving Belvoir I should do the same. I went on following in my father's footsteps, by going to work in the Belfast shipyard, just as he had followed his father into Harland and Wolff. We had our own traditions to follow, just as they do in England. There a man goes to school at Eton and his sons will go there. He goes to Oxford, or Cambridge, and his sons consequently do likewise. A father is a famous politician, and nine times out of ten one of the sons finishes up in politics. But for me it was Mersey Street School, and then the shipyard. If I had been interested in furthering my academic career, we would have had to have the money to push me through four or five extra years at school.

It's strange how little one can sometimes remember about one's parents, even when you live together. The way it was with us, all I can remember of my father from those days is his getting up in the morning, working all day, coming home at night, having his dinner or tea, followed by a wash and shave. Then he would go out and wouldn't come back till ten or eleven at night. I presume he spent his leisure hours in pubs, because most men in the district I was born in went out drinking every night. So, all in all, I never saw much of my father.

The main things I remember are that he had a very pleasant if dominating personality and that, then as now, he was a very funny man. He was once a notable sprinter and was very quick off the mark. I suppose he passed this athletic prowess on to me. I do remember racing my father for about a hundred yards from the top of Avon Street to where we lived; he was about forty years of age and I was about thirteen or fourteen years old. But looking back upon it we didn't spend much time with each other, because he was working every day and all day. I don't remember my father ever missing a day of work, which was a wonderful record. He was one of those who always wanted to work because he had a family to support, and he also wanted a bit of money to spend on his own pleasures.

My father was a boilermaker in the shipyard and he was a specialist in the riveting department. The man in charge of riveting had a squad to work under him. This included the "holder-up", the "heater boy", and the "catch boy". (There was one "holder-up" who was remembered for a long time, but not because he was a "holder-up". This was Willie Houston, who played for Linfield for many years and who was an international player some forty years ago.)

I know that for a long time I was the favourite in the family, because I had three sisters and I was the only boy until, later on, two younger brothers came along. My father was very unselfish to me. He gave me many things and encouraged me to take up different sports. For a time I was very interested in boxing. Money was pretty short but he gave me enough to buy a complete outfit to go and train.

It's only in the last ten years that I have realised how important the woman is in the family. It was my mother who held our family together; more so than my father. She was a woman of tremendous courage, and tremendous strength—a woman completely dedicated to bringing up her family. She sacrificed her life to this. She rarely went out and I think that her only luxury was going to the pictures once a week. She was very good friends with my Aunt Sadie, and they used to see each other every Saturday and spend the evening together. When, in present days, I think about "Women's

Liberation", I wish it could have come, say, twenty years ago; particularly in Ulster where I am certain women on the whole had a raw deal. The men there probably got more freedom than any other men that I have come across in my life. But the women were indoctrinated that the only way of life for them was to care for their family. I always thought this place of the women in Ulster only held within the Protestant community. But later when I was friendly with a couple of Catholics and went often to their houses, I saw the situation was just the same with them. So I find that both Catholic and Protestant were prisoners of the same environment.

Living next door to my grandmother, as I did for such a long time, I became aware of two different types of woman. My grandmother was one type, and my mother, especially from the cooking angle, was another. My grandmother dealt with little things and intricate cooking, like home-made bread, home-made cakes, scones, and with the fresh butter bit. My mother was one for cooking substantial food—like Irish stew.

When I look back on it, Irish stew was as tasty as similar dishes throughout Europe. In England and even in America wherever I have ordered goulash (a great favourite of mine) it has tasted an awful lot like Irish stew. I don't know if chefs have had the same recipe for Irish stew all over Europe and the U.S.A. and transformed it into goulash. I expect it originated as a country dish, for it consists of great chunks of all kinds of meat engulfed with vegetables and with a lot of potatoes thrown in. It is then boiled for quite some time on the stove. Another dish we used to have, on a Sunday, was a joint of meat. This came once a week—every Sunday the same. It was a large joint and we would have what remained in sandwiches for high tea later in the day. And if there was anything left over my mother (I don't know how she managed to do it all) made it the foundation for a great big soup-cum-stew for Monday night.

The Catholics always went to Mass on Sunday. The top end of Newtownards Road would be full of people all morning, and all evening you would have the Protestant community of the Newtownards Road dressed up in their best clothes and going to Bible Class (held morning, afternoon, and night). The Catholics and the Protestants always congregated in church or in Sunday School all day Sundays. Sunday was a very religious day. It was a special day for other reasons, like having the joint of meat, or visiting. For me Sunday was the start of a new week, and I always looked forward to a Sunday afternoon between about two and six or seven o'clock when I would go and spend many relaxing and leisurely hours with my aunt and uncle up in Thistle Street, playing cards.

When you were old enough to take part in any kind of communal activity it seems now that it was either playing football or some other out-of-doors game, or playing cards. Under some circumstances even card-playing was an out-of-doors exercise. My love for cards started way back when I was about eight or nine years old, and I was induced to play because everyone else round our street used to be involved, from six-year-olds up to, say, forty-year-olds. I learned the game simply by watching my elders play, and then I was able to go through the games and play with the younger boys. By the time that I was twelve or thirteen years of age I was good enough to play cards with the older boys, and we played for hours and hours in the evenings. We congregated at the top of Medway Street, because the light was pretty good there. First we played by gaslight. Some nights the light was worse than others because some boys pinched the mantles for use at home. Later on, however, electric light was installed. Cards weren't too expensive, and we didn't play for high stakes because there wasn't much money around. We played an awful lot of poker, and I sometimes made a bit of money. We also played a great game called "Partner Whist", which is on the lines of Bridge, and

"Solo", and if the money was flowing, we played three-card brag. All of this is still going on even twenty-five years later. years later.

Looking back one cannot help but wonder why grown men and young boys should play cards seven days a week, every week in the year, every year being the same as the one before. As I said, over there nothing seems to change.

You could go out of Belfast, Northern Ireland, Ulster, and come back ten years later. If it wasn't the same guys who were hanging round the same corner it would be those who had taken their places. They all looked alike anyway. There is an all too familiar and tragic set of circumstances behind this. A man wakes up in the morning with nothing to do, and no job to go to. He relies on social security and other government benefits and has to play cards all day.

Near the bottom of Dee Street (just under the Dee Street railway bridge that used to be there) there was a betting office, and in between races young men who were out of work used to drift across there and put their sixpences and shillings on their fancies. Then back to the cards. This was a ritual for them.

The Irish—whether northern or southern, Catholic or Protestant—have a great gambling streak in them and this seems to have been going on for ever. When I mixed more with Catholics later on, they told me how exactly the same thing happened in their district from Sunday to Sunday, week to week, and year to year, as in ours. Cards was a great occupation participated in by young and old, Catholic and Protestant.

Another occupation that both sets of the community had in common was fighting. Every Friday and Saturday there used always to be two or three fights a night. This was a sort of end of week procedure in which brothers, and cousins and uncles would go out drinking together all evening. And there would often be some discontent among them which would break out into fisticuffs. It wasn't uncommon to see a fight

either in Medway Street or Avon Street, or on the bottom of
Dee Street, or on one of the other nearby watery streets,
with thirty or forty people watching.

It seemed to be the only way that one could settle an
argument. But there are worse ways. I have seen men stand
for a long time squaring up at each other, and at last come to
blows, which they thought right, fit and proper at that
particular time. So I suppose there is some truth in the
opinion that Irishmen—all Irishmen—love a good fight.

It's funny when I look back upon it, but I can't ever
remember when I saw a policeman come off his beat on the
Newtownards Road, come down Dee Street, and eventually
down Avon Street or Medway Street. This seems—looking
back—rather an alarming fact.

A great experience for me was something as simple as
catching a bus into town and having a walk round the centre
of Belfast. It was a marvellous couple of hours for me on a
Saturday morning. When I lived on the east side of Belfast I
always had the opinion that all the best people lived up the
Knock or the Malone Roads. I never challenged this, because
of the influence of parents and grandparents. If you lived in
one environment you thought like everyone else in the same
environment. In Avon Street you could only accept a
situation, you couldn't change it. And you did this easily and
readily. I remember travelling on Belfast buses for more
reasons than one. On the buses I would come across boys
from other parts of the city. As I listened to their talk I
detected that they spoke with a different brogue from me.
Their voices seemed more refined. I thought this was rather
strange, because up until then I thought that everyone in
Belfast spoke the same—well, all the Protestants anyway. I
never remember discussing Catholics until I was about eleven
or twelve years old which was when I first came across them.

I first heard about anything outside Belfast or Northern
Ireland when my father told me about the time he worked in
Glasgow during the war; I thought Glasgow seemed like a

different world away from me. And London was so remote, so far away from Belfast, that the only way that I could hear or see anything about it was by going to the pictures and watching the News. That gave you a complete round-up of all the events of the week in about five or ten minutes—and that was my only form of information.

What I did know about London, and would take for granted, was that Buckingham Palace was the home of the Royal Family. The home of Winston Churchill was also in London, and we were reminded of these facts by the portraits hanging in school. Great houses far away, and portraits of great people who lived in these great houses. There was the King of England, or the Queen, or Winston Churchill. There were pictures of Churchill that seemed almost lifesize. We were very proud of all these things for some reason or other. Just as were all the people in east Belfast who had such portraits hanging in their houses. This or that picture did an awful lot to develop one's loyalty. I didn't know then that other people had other pictures and other loyalties. In Avon Street and thereabouts we stayed put with "God save the King".

Going on from this, another part of my childhood and background was the "Twelfth"—the 12th July. As a matter of fact I always looked forward to the eleventh more than the "Twelfth" because as I didn't go on the Orange Day marches we used to have a big bonfire the night before the great day. All the boys from Avon and every neighbouring Street would collect all the old tyres and wood that could be found and we would have this huge bonfire on the wasteground at the bottom of Dee Street, for which my mother would let me stay up all night. Sitting around the bonfire, we would roast potatoes and have lots of other things to eat, which made it more memorable for me than the Orangemen's walk to Finaghy.

I now realise how lucky I was to have had such a mother, who had such a great influence on my childhood. It was her discipline that probably stopped me getting involved with the young boys round our district—and there were a lot of them—who did nothing else but get into trouble with the police. They broke the law, probably every day, mostly by petty stealing and breaking into shops. That I didn't go that way was because of my mother. She never stopped me from going with them, but she said that if I did the same as them and broke the law, and if the police came to our house, she would say, "I am not going to ask the police what you have done. I will say: There he is and you can take him away from me." That stayed in my mind and it has remained there ever since.

Although my mother was a very small woman, just over five feet, she had tremendous strength of character. I hope that a little of this may have rubbed off on me.

When my mother died—I was about sixteen—a part of me died too. But I did not realise this until about twelve months afterwards, when the effect on a family of losing a mother became clear. The mother is the most important one in the family. She is irreplaceable.

It was then that I decided that Ulster was not for me. I had to be lucky enough to use my football skill—such as it then was—to find a team who could transfer me to somewhere "across the water". As it happened when the time came there were a number of English clubs who were interested in me. Football was my only outlet, my only means of getting away. What did I want to get away from? I'm not sure that it had taken any kind of definite shape in my mind.

But I had been playing also with other ideas of getting away from Northern Ireland. Two of my great-uncles had emigrated to America. My father, I knew, had a friend who lived there, and there was a cousin who lived there as well. I had watched so many American films that I already had a good impression of life there.

"Fat Joe", my father's friend, went from Ireland well over twenty years ago. And every week for twenty years, my father sent him the *Weekend News, Reveille,* and the *Ulster Saturday Night*—the fullest sports paper one could ever see.

"Fat Joe" Hamilton came from Lurgan and he worked with my father as an apprentice riveter. He didn't see much future in a lifetime of riveting, and going away from Ulster was the best thing he ever did. He went to Exeter, New Hampshire, and became a Sergeant Cook in the U.S. Army. But he liked to keep hold of old memories, and so he looked to getting the papers every week from "home".

My Aunt Sadie's son, Trevor McNeelly, was always one of my favourite male cousins. He went to America and also did well for himself. He now lives in Atlanta, Georgia, and is some sort of personnel manager for the United States Government.

What with films and the names like Murphy that kept cropping up, and the fantasy of it all, and the impression that America was a second home—a foster-home—of Irish people, I always felt its appeal. I often used to talk with my aunts, particularly with Aunt Sadie, and wondered about the possibility that when I was older—sixteen, seventeen, or eighteen—we could all go to America.

But the real thing was playing football. After Mr. Mawhinney saw me playing and thought I might make a footballer, there was the problem of finding me a pair of football boots. I never forget the first pair I had. They were about two sizes too large for me and I borrowed them from a fellow called Billy Dickie. The first competitive game I ever played was for the junior side. In that particular match we drew, one each, and I had the good fortune to score a goal. Soon in that game I did something that I did not realise I was doing: playing at centre-forward I kept dropping back, and the centre-half kept going up. After we had talked about that particular match Mr. Mawhinney decided to put me at centre-half and he put a boy called Joe Martin at centre-forward. That was a "tactical switch" which remained with me for the next three years, and when I played for the

Minors, the Juniors, and the Seniors it was as a centre-half. My father, who then told me to take football seriously, bought me my first pair of boots. At that time I was ten years old.

When I look back now I know how much I owe to Mr. Mawhinney for encouraging me to take up football. It is hard to realise how much I practised—sometimes four, sometimes six, sometimes even eight hours a day. When I say practise I include playing the actual game with the boys around my own age at the top of Avon Street. A favourite exercise of mine was to pick up a small rubber ball and head it up against the side of a house. In fact we had a competition amongst us to see who could keep the ball going a thousand times. I saw many good players on the cobbled streets, on concrete, or on waste ground, and I used to try to imitate the style and control of the best boys. I began to develop my own style, which, I think, in some ways is unique. Learning to play where we did, and how we did, taught you to stand on your own feet—if you were lucky.

My gymnasium was Avon Street. At the bottom of Avon Street was a patch of waste ground which we called the "Meadow"—there is a brewery there now—and on Sundays we would be out there as early as nine o'clock in the morning. We would start with two or three on each side, and by lunch time, we probably had as many as twelve or fourteen a side. Then for the next two hours it fluctuated, with people (boys and even grown-up men) going for their dinner (or their lunch). This went on until dusk, and even beyond, so that sometimes the game lasted up to twelve hours.

I would have to go to Sunday School for about a couple of hours. I would go home and change into my best clothes and then change back after Sunday School. Then I would dash back to the "Meadow" where I would find the score something like forty-two to thirty-seven. Such was my Sunday.

We never changed to play football. We played in our second-best togs, but fortunately since I wasn't ever a goal-keeper I never got my clothes too dirty. The only thing I ruined was my shoes, and I seemed to go through a pair a month, which was rather expensive. But my mother didn't seem to mind too much. I said I wasn't a goal-keeper. As a matter of fact we didn't have one. Anyone defended the goal which in any case was a very makeshift affair. We never had a referee either, or any linesman. It was the sort of game in which if one said it was a goal, it was. We played to our own rules, and we knew after playing week in and week out which rule would stand and which wouldn't.

Of those who played, I now recall the Leamans—Dickie, Harry and Billy—the Beatties, "Skinny" Watson, "Stew" Agnew, and Harold Pickering. Harold was a very close friend of mine when I was about thirteen or fourteen years old. All the men and boys were one hundred per cent Protestant. Within our area, which was a couple of miles square, there wasn't a single Catholic living.

The first time I came across a Catholic would have been when I was eleven years old, and I was playing centre-half for Mersey Street School. We were drawn in the Belfast Schools' Cup, and played a team from Ardoyne—a Catholic School. That was the first time that I actually saw or came in contact in any way with a Roman Catholic boy. It was also the first time I saw a couple of priests. We were very lucky that day to draw one all. But when we brought that team back to Victoria Park we completely overwhelmed them. I believe the score was seven-one or seven-nil. So we went on to the next round of that Cup.

4

"The stand gutted, the grass growing wild"

When I left Mersey Street School I went to the Belfast Technical High School. The reason for my going to the Technical High School was that I had been born in January! Normally I would have had to leave school at the end of the term that finished in March. That would have prevented me playing for the Irish Schools international team, in which I had a fair chance of playing. The previous year it was decided at school that I should sit an exam for entrance to the Technical High School. I was lucky enough to pass and so could stay on at school until the end of June. I played the three international matches in April and May, against England, Scotland and Wales.

Going to Belfast Technical High School for twelve months was a marvellous experience in itself, because it educated me in the lay-out and character of the City. I had to catch a bus that went over the Queen's Bridge, round by the docks, and right through the city centre itself. I got off at the City Hall, and walked past the Athletic Stores and arrived at the school. This was next door to the Belfast Academical Institution and two hundred yards up the road was the grand old Opera House. Next door to that was the Great Northern Railway station. If you wanted to go to the Republic (or to Eire, or to Southern Ireland, whatever you called that part of Ireland), you caught all the trains there. I didn't know this until I went to the Technical High School.

This was the first fime that I had really to conform, for I

had to wear a special uniform. My mother, of course, had to sacrifice to buy me this. I was very tall when I was thirteen, standing about five feet seven or five feet eight inches tall. I only went and got the uniform on condition that my mother bought me long trousers with it!

If you were a schoolboy aged thirteen you could travel at half fare. I always had great difficulty in persuading any bus conductor that I was under fourteen, and, to do so, I had to wear my school cap all the time. I didn't like wearing this but, as we couldn't afford full fare, I had to wear it to enable me to get to and from school. Instead of having lunch at school, I had it with my mother because we had an hour and a half's break. I used to dash from school back to the City Hall to catch the bus home. This meant that I had to catch four buses a day, so I had four different conductors to tell the same story to—about being under fourteen so could I travel for half the fare?

The difference between Mersey Street and the Tech. was that in Mersey Street we had the same teacher teaching us for all subjects. At the High School we had three quite new subjects—science, French, and woodwork—with a special teacher for each. This in itself was a great experience. It was also strange to be in a building where there were no small boys under the age of thirteen. There were very big boys getting on for twenty, who were there for six or seven years to try and finish their matriculation.

I came across a lot of boys who eventually made a success for themselves after they had left the High School. Two who were famous before I arrived at the High School and who had made their mark on English and Irish international football were the former captain of Ireland and Tottenham Hotspur, Danny Blanchflower, and Billy Bingham. Billy was one of my heroes when I was at Mersey Street School and he was playing for Glentoran Football Club. He finished up by being the most capped player of all time for Ireland, after which he became the manager of the Northern Ireland team.

My only reason for going to Belfast High was to further my footballing career. I only found out by accident, two or three months after I had left school, that if I had passed my exam I could have stayed on the next year. I could probably have stayed on anyway despite exam results, but I wasn't all that interested. My aunt told me that my mother wanted me to stay on and that my mother told her that if I had passed the exam I would have had a brand new bicycle. Later on in England I learned that it was quite the custom to bribe children to "do well at school". It can't be said that my mother was guilty of this. Anyway I don't know how she could have afforded a new bicycle. The whole thing came out from Aunt Belle—the one in Thistle Street.

There was, however, one good reason for leaving school. This was a reason that cut short the education of many boys, and still does. It is the most compelling of all reasons: money, or rather, not having any. I knew that if I left school I could get some sort of job which would give me pocket money and my mother an extra pound or two to help her look after the running of the house. All the boys I knew of my own age had already left school and I felt envious of them. They not only didn't have to go to school but had money to go to the pictures with, and to buy new clothes. So I said, "Right, I'll leave." And I left.

In my High School year I played against Wales in Cardiff and against England at York. In the Northern Irish schoolboy team there was a mixture both of talent and of background. Two or three of the players were Catholic—but those of us who weren't had a respect for their football and that was a good enough reason for thinking other things unimportant. Sammy McQuee was from Bangor, and played at centre-forward or inside-forward. He was outstanding. One of the Catholic boys was called McGuire: I'm certain he came from the Ardoyne district, which I then knew to be a Roman Catholic area. Another very skilful player was Jim Cairns. My best friend from this team was a goal-keeper—Jim

Dobbin.

It is remarkable as I look back to realise that at least half the players in the side were far better than me. It is one of those imponderables—I just cannot work it out—that talent which shows at fourteen, fifteen, or sixteen can stagnate and stop developing. I wish I could find the answer to that question which is not only one that applies to football.

If I had not been picked for the schoolboy international team I would never have ventured outside Ireland, or even Belfast. I don't remember that I had ever before been anywhere else, with the exception of Bangor or Holywood, but I really considered these places were parts of greater Belfast. A once famous international player named Priestley, who used to play for Chelsea and Northern Ireland, was in charge of the Irish team. (He was a schoolmaster and is now headmaster of a school in Lisburn.) One thing I remember clearly from those two trips, to Wales and to England, was that all the players had in common an addiction to playing cards. We played poker all night on the cross-channel boat going over and all night coming back. We weren't too excited about the trip "across the water". What mattered was how many shillings we won at cards.

I didn't think that my twelve months at the Technical High was wasted, but I do regret now not taking enough interest in my academic studies. When I went there, of course, the only thing that was on my mind was becoming an Irish schoolboy international. I had already made up my mind that I wanted to have a career as a footballer. Not necessarily as a professional footballer, but one with a decent reputation. What helped to drive me on was that I was the first boy from the east side of Belfast to be capped as a schoolboy player for a very long time. This was something I am certain that my mother and my father were very proud of.

The one home match that we played that year was against Scotland at Grosvenor Park. When I played at Grosvenor

Park, the home of Distillery Football Club, that night, I
never realised how important the next three or four years, in
which I played regularly up at the Grosvenor Road, would
be. I never realised how much bearing it would have on my
life.

Fifteen years later, I went back to Belfast to play for my
country in an international match against Russia. During my
stay in Belfast I went along to see again what had happened
to Grosvenor Park (which is in Distillery Street). It was a
very sad experience for me to see the stand gutted, the grass
growing wild—all completely run down. When I saw the
bathrooms and the dressing-rooms in the place where I had
had such wonderful years I had an empty feeling and a
sadness. Part of my life which always lingers inside me was
brought to mind again. I thought of all the people I would
never see or hear of again. This was a feeling of utter despair,
for it was Grosvenor Park and the Distillery Football Club
that set me on the road that took me over to England.

While I was at the ground that day there were four of five
young boys there. Suddenly, when they saw the television
camera there, they came running over. They thought that we
were intruders, but when they recognised me they quickly
asked if they could come on TV. As we were setting
ourselves up for an item at the far end of the ground one of
the boys asked if I would hold his transistor radio which he
had been listening to. These boys were between the ages of
nine and fourteen. They should have been in school, but
they confessed quite without shame that they were in the
habit of "mitching school".

I asked them what had been happening. They told me that
the soldiers had stopped them from fighting with the
"Orange bastards". When they said "Orange bastards" this
intrigued me because they didn't realise they were speaking
to a Protestant. I said, "Well, what do you mean by 'Orange
bastards'?" He said, "The 'Orange bastards' are always
fighting with us." I asked them to describe how it all started

in 1969. Bearing in mind that these boys were very young
and that was nearly three years ago, it was frightening that
they had ideas such as they had. I continued my questioning
and asked them if they couldn't live in harmony and peace
with the Orange people. They said, "Oh, they don't want it.
They are always creating trouble for us." If I spoke to the
"Orange bastards"—as they called them—they would probably tell me the same story, only this time the bastards
would not be the Orange but Fenian. And this is the problem
in Belfast, if you speak to one side of the community you get
a slanted view, regardless of which side you speak to. It is not
surprising that the British Army stated that they come across
young boys of between ten and fourteen with guns in their
hands. Those small boys to whom I spoke and whom I asked
if they found the intrusion of the army exciting said, "Yes,
we find it very exciting." One said, "We saw a couple of
people shot last week, and it is so exciting with all the bullets
flying. I hear the bullets every night, and I hear explosions."
For them, it was like all the fiction and fantasy films coming
to life.

It was, I thought, different when I was that age. But it is
men who are of my age, and older, who are stirring the old
troubles afresh. Who is to blame for what? You can't get out
of things by saying, "it was different in my day!"

After I left the Technical High School I had a job in the
Triang factory—a toy factory owned by an English firm,
Lines Brothers—on the Castlereagh Road. I might, of course,
have stayed there. If I had stayed long enough I would have
been rewarded with unemployment in the end. The Triang
firm eventually went broke through economic circumstances in England and political troubles in Ulster. Anyway I
spent eighteen months working there. I did numerous jobs
from putting tyres onto the wheels of prams, both small ones
and big ones, to helping supply all the different parts and
pieces to make up different toys. Scooters, prams, bicycles,
and so on. I also helped with the stuffing of various toy

animals. I found it more exciting working there than in the shipyard, where I was to go next, because of the variety of work in a toy factory. Of course the novelty of getting £4 or £5 a week was a great incentive for me. As I was not yet fifteen I could not officially work overtime. But I was fortunate; I got on very well with the foreman and he let me work overtime.

So far as football was concerned I had the opportunity to play with men and older boys. When we had finished lunch we used to play for about half an hour during the break. But I needed the organisation of competitive football, and Mersey Street Boys' Club, of which I was a member, closed down for some reason or other. There were only two opportunities for me to have competitive football, either by joining the Boyland Youth Club or the Cregagh Boys' Club. I decided to join the latter because I thought there would be a better chance of getting regular games. As a schoolboy international, even though I was only a fourteen-year-old, I had a minor reputation.

Joining the Cregagh Boys' Club meant about thirty minutes travelling by bus. If I went by bike—I had one then—it took about twenty minutes. The leader of the Club was a Mr. Stafford Young and there were other activities than football. I used to play billiards and table tennis there and in this way showed a general interest. Unless you did, you weren't chosen to play football.

These two years were a great period for me. When I went to the Belfast Tech. I had finished playing as a centre-half and I got a bee in my bonnet about playing in the forward line. I played centre-forward in a very good team and scored a lot of goals—which helped me to get selected for the schoolboy international team. When I joined Cregagh Boys' Club I had a great obsession to play inside-left, and I was lucky enough to be able to keep a regular place in the "Under 15" side as an inside-left. The field we played on was in the estate of Cregagh, and every Saturday morning the older boys of the club had to put out the goal-posts to enable the match to take place. The other teams that we played were boys' clubs from all over Belfast. I don't *know* if we played against Roman Catholics, but I am pretty certain that we didn't. The reason why I say I am pretty certain is that most Roman Catholic boys who are keen on football are always encouraged to play the "national game" of Ireland. As far as Eire goes this is Gaelic football. I have met a number of Irish soccer players who started this way. Martin O'Neill, who has broken into the international team, was playing Gaelic football until he changed over, and within fifteen months he was transferred to Nottingham Forest. They paid £15,000 for him.

Another thing different about playing football in Belfast was that it went on virtually for twelve months in the year. We played in friendlies and then the Boys' Club League from September to the following May, and then in "Summer football". The nice thing about football in summer was that you were always going out on pleasant evenings—mostly down Victoria Park. But since I played football all the year round I never played any sort of cricket. Many English football clubs—like Wolves, West Bromwich Albion, and Manchester United and City—do have cricket matches amongst themselves. These are often for charity. But I have never been able to take part. As I look back I find it rather sad that I couldn't play either cricket or Rugby football at Mersey Street School. It was football—"soccer"—or nothing. I have never heard of anybody from Mersey Street actually being selected for the Irish rugby team, and the same goes for cricket. There have been plenty of outstanding Irish cricketers—though probably not as good as English cricketers—but they came from another school system than ours.

In some ways it is embarrassing not to be able to play cricket, and it makes me uncomfortable when I can't bowl out my eight-year-old son. All these reasons add up to make me feel that Northern Ireland is a country on its own. I certainly could never visualise Northern Ireland v Australians, or West Indians; cricket is just not a national game, but is one that the top-class people, the elite, of Belfast play.

In England I have met and been involved with a lot of rugby players—top rugby players. When you get talking with them they sometimes say something like, "Oh, I have played a little soccer". But I have never been able to say, "Oh, I have played a little rugger", due to the difference of background. On the whole I prefer Rugby League which is a faster game. I would, perhaps, fancy myself as using my sprinting ability and being one of those players who make spectacular tries!

As it was I played soccer all the time. I think about the days in Victoria Park, the games in the Summer League and, above all, the matches at the "Hen Run"—Wilgar Park, the home of Dundela F.C.

It is amazing how important Boys' Club football was in Belfast. It reared many prominent Irish internationals and famous English and Scottish League club players. Players of note who came from Boyland Youth Club were Jimmy Nicholson and Jacky Scott. The greatest player after my time who came from Cregagh was, of course, George Best.

When I was with Cregagh Boys' Club, I signed for Distillery Football Club. I was fifteen years old at this particular point, but I already had some connection with two other clubs in Belfast. Linfield had signed me when I was fourteen and I went up to Windsor Park and trained religiously, two nights a week, for months and months. I didn't make any progress and didn't play for any of their teams and I left, rather disillusioned. I was, however, playing well for the Boys' Club team at the time. I was captain, and my position was inside-left. I had once set my heart on playing for the Glens because I followed them devoutly for years and years; ever since I was ten, in fact. Coming from the east side of Belfast, I thought it should be my ambition to play for Glentoran. They sent a scout to watch me and he reported that I wasn't a bad ball player. But I couldn't make their fourth team, which was rather ironical, because a couple of years later I was playing against the Glens in the Irish Cup Final when I was on the winning side and got an Irish Cup winner's medal. One of the reasons why I was emotionally involved with the Glentoran ground was that just after the war, about 1946, I used to go there with some of my school friends to catch tadpoles and, as we called them, "smicks". The Oval then was one large bomb-site with craters—the result of what was inflicted on "loyal Ulster" because of its Britishness and its wartime value to Britain. In a few years it was transformed back to a football ground, with thousands of people coming to watch. In those years I got the bug for playing football, and when I went back to the Oval as a thirteen-year-old I couldn't believe what had happened.

Where I had spent a number of years as a seven-year-old catching tadpoles and "smicks", suddenly there were twenty-two men running about and performing with virtuosity and artistry. It was a built-in nostalgic feeling, a feeling of great sentiment, to see all this coming about within a few years. When I was a little boy I had five heroes, Sammy Lowry, Sammy Ewing, Sammy Hughes, Tim Williamson, and outside-left "Dado" Feeney, from Londonderry. When I was watching those "famous five" playing, I had the impression—and it stayed with me for a long, long time—that Sammy Lowry was the most fantastic outside-right I have ever seen. Sammy Ewing was the best "killer" of the ball with his chest that I had ever seen. I never saw Tommy Lawton or the equally famous "Dixie" Dean play, but I am certain that if I had I would still have wished that I could head a ball like Sammy Hughes. Even to this day, I sometimes wish that. Surely Sammy Hughes was the most brilliant header of the ball I have seen in my life.

Distillery F.C., which I joined when I was fifteen, had a manager then called Jimmy Macintosh, the former Blackpool and Preston Scottish international. Distillery Street lies off the Grosvenor Road, and the football ground is situated at the bottom. Behind it, the Distillery itself produces Irish Whiskey (not Scottish, Whisky). It is also situated not too far from the Falls Road which borders on both Protestant and Catholic communities, and those teams that I played for in the middle fifties were mixed sides of Protestant and Catholic players. We also had two or three Scots over, and even they were mixed—Scottish Protestant and Scottish Catholic. I certainly never found any problem with religion in my Distillery days. We had mixed sets of players and we also had a mixed set of spectators, coming from both areas. I can't remember any sort of trouble involving the two sides of the community in those days, and it's pleasant to look back especially with the situation as it now is.

When I was playing for Distillery—a "mixed" team—Linfield were firm in ruling that everyone employed by that Club should be Protestant. In early days Ulster was largely Scottish, its settlers of, say, three hundred years ago nearly all coming from Scotland, hence names of streets near our house like Thistle Street. So far as football is concerned Linfield follow the same traditions as Glasgow Rangers and even play in exactly the same colours.

It is ironical how things have worked out for me because the situation could have been reversed and I could have been playing for Linfield after all. When I was prominent as an amateur player, and holding my place in Distillery Football Club, I know for a fact that I could have signed as a professional for Linfield. One team that I don't remember much about, apart from what I have been told, was Belfast Celtic. They were mainly a Catholic stronghold, and they played at Celtic Park in Catholic surroundings. They had to go out of existence in the late forties for political reasons.

My first game for Distillery was about my sixteenth birthday, when I played against Glenavon in the Irish Cup. I suppose when you are always used to playing in front of a handful of spectators any real "gate" looks big. The gate I played in front of that day was about £300! This way of putting it seems rather strange to anyone living outside Belfast, but that was how they judged the crowd there. They didn't say it was 5,000 or 10,000 people watching today, they said that the gate money was £300 or £600. In Ulster the money that was taken at a match seemed more important than the number of people who watched.

The nickname for Distillery was the "Lilywhites", the reason being that we played in white jerseys and black knickers—the same colours then as Preston North End, Tottenham Hotspur and the English international team. Looking back our colours seem to have been more or less "neutral" amid those that aroused more of love and hate.

All that seems far, far away when I remember my visit to Grosvenor Park in October 1971, on the day before Northern Ireland played Russia. I went from the city centre, up the Grosvenor Road and down Distillery Street, with the military all around. I remember how the Oval had been destroyed by the known enemy during the last world war. I saw what remained of Distillery Football Club from the vicious actions of an unknown enemy. But on the bit of stand that was still there I read in clear, large letters: "Distillery F.C., 1879". So long was the tradition that had gone up in smoke.

5

"An apprentice had to start somewhere"

When I went to Distillery, I found myself playing in the third team as centre-forward or inside-left, and I remember scoring three goals in my first match against Chimney Corner—an amateur team which one would probably find somewhere in County Antrim. I did enough to impress the club after a few games that I was worth a place in the reserves. Here I used to get fifteen shillings a week; it was put down as expenses, and I suppose in a way it was because I was a few shillings a week out of pocket for bus fares to Grosvenor Park for training sessions and games. I was lucky, I only played so few times in the third team.

It was a great experience to be in the reserves and it was a marvellous foundation to my career. I played in three or four positions in the forward line, mostly at outside-left. My grandfather—my first critic—had long before said that I was all left foot. The teams I played against included Ballyclare Comrades, Newry Town, Larne, and Banbridge Town, as well as city teams. That January, when I was sixteen, I was chosen for Distillery's first team to play against Glenavon in the Irish Cup at centre-forward. When I was selected I was flabbergasted. I remember clearly that the Glenavon team that day included the legendary Wilbur Cush, late of Leeds United, and Jimmy Jones who had played in the troubled match which ended the life of Celtic F.C. It was an important match for the Whites, as well as me, since Glenavon was the outstanding team of that time. We were rather unlucky not to win the game, which finished as a draw with no goals. On the following Wednesday, however, we were beaten by three clear goals in Lurgan.

I think I played one or two more matches and then I was dropped back into the reserves. Until the end of the season I played in and out of the first team making about twelve appearances. Playing for Distillery also added to my experience as a native of Northern Ireland and Belfast. I travelled to Ballyclare in Antrim, where there were bleaching works; to Banbridge, a rather fine market town in Co. Down; and to the border town of Newry. All this travelling outside of Belfast for the first time in my life was really marvellous. I have later learned how much one gains through travel; but one should never neglect to get to know one's own country.

The first time I ever went to Londonderry, of course, was to play football, and when I first played there for Distillery was the first time I saw "Derry's Walls". The nickname of the Derry ground always amused me; it was Brandywell! Now Derry City, like Distillery, and for the same reason, are not to be seen at home, having to play "home" matches away.

At Coleraine, a clean town on the Bann before you get to Derry, the football club played on the "Showground". Ballymena had a ground with that name too. In both places, as the names tell us, horses and cattle appeared as well as footballers! I liked the name of the Glenavon ground, which was Mourne View, because of the Mourne Mountains—although these were not all that near.

My first season with Distillery ended with the manager, Jimmy Macintosh, leaving the club, and the appointment of Maurice Tadman, the former Plymouth and Charlton footballer, who came over and had the title of player-manager. I found that working under Mr. Tadman was very good for me because we got on well together.

My inconsistency in the previous six months, in and out of the team, was because I knew that I could play more consistently as centre-half or left-half. When I was a schoolboy playing in a half-back role I found that all the glamour and all the publicity was for forward players and as I had the ability, ball control, and general skill to play in the forward line I was happy to stay there. After I left the schoolboy internationals, I concentrated on the inside-left position where you always seem to be in the thick of things.

Until I joined Distillery I didn't realise that the gulf between playing in a Boys' Club League, or even in top amateur football, and playing with professionals was so great. It was a different world for me. I thought it would be just as easy for me to play in the Distillery first team at centre-forward or inside-forward as it had been in junior club football. But I soon learned that I couldn't put on the same kind of performances playing in the best professional football (such as it was) in Northern Ireland.

When Maurice Tadman came I thought that I would be much better playing as a defender at wing-half. It was at this time that I began to know what this game of football was all about. To me it was about playing as well as your ability would let you. And I thought that if I couldn't play as naturally and as consistently in the forward line as I could as a defender, I would ask Mr. Tadman to give me the opportunity to play at wing-half. I would rather have played consistently in the second team than have inconsistent performances in the first team. When I talked to Mr. Tadman he understood my problems and when he had listened to them he gave me the opportunity. But there were certain occasions when he would talk to me and say, "Well, this week I'd rather you played inside-forward in the first team." In this respect I can now see that it was his use of psychology, his way of getting through to me; and it seemed to bring out the best in me. Fortunately enough for the next two or three years I played in whatever position Mr. Tadman wanted me to. But usually I was a centre-half or a left-half, and it was from there that I became one of the youngest captains of Distillery Football Club. One thing that I can quite categorically state is that I never had an individual coaching session in my life. I have always been self-taught and had more or less mimicked other footballers since I was ten years of age. I also developed a lot of probably bad habits which I found it hard to get rid of even under the more or less disciplined training we had when Mr. Tadman came. He himself solved our centre-forward spot when he came. He was still a useful player in that position and experience can be a wonderful asset when properly employed. The boss went on to score many vital goals for Distillery in those days. I was relieved because I thought, "Well, that's one position I shan't be playing in, because the boss plays there himself." There were two positions at that time I was not keen on, centre-forward and right-back. The only positions I never filled at Distillery were right-back and goalkeeper.

One player who was to make a great impact on English football in more ways than one and who also played in Northern Ireland at that time was George Eastham. He was English but his father was the manager of Ards F.C. I must say here that I always admired the elder Eastham for the "push and run" style that he introduced from England into Northern Ireland. The younger George was transferred from Ards to Newcastle United in 1956.

In the Irish League we only used to have regular training on Tuesday and Thursday nights—after being at work all day. Twenty years later the Irish part-timers can still only train on Tuesdays and Thursdays. Here is something else in Northern Ireland that hasn't altered in my lifetime.

There were, it seems, many differences between Northern Ireland and England and one of the main ones so far as I was concerned was that I couldn't become a full-time professional footballer in Northern Ireland. In England, on the other hand, with its ninety-two League clubs, one has the opportunity to become a full-time professional footballer. In Northern Ireland there wasn't the money to finance either the clubs or the players in a full-time capacity like there is in

England. So I had to look for a profession.

As my grandfather worked in the shipyard, and my father worked in the shipyard, my mother decided that my future lay in the shipyard as well, and I was never asked about it. They decided I should be an electrician.

Why I became an electrician is a bit obscure. It seems to have had something to do with pigeons. Like my grandfather Dougan, my father was a keen fancier. He says that one day I went down to the Island to fetch his pigeons and that for some reason or other I then decided I would not become a riveter. So I became an electrician by whim.

My first day in the shipyard I had to be there at eight o'clock. My mother made up my lunch for me in my lunch-box and when I went down there my father showed me where the offices were to which I had to report. I gave my name and was sent to a gentleman who seemed to know all about me. I remember that as well as my lunch I had to take with me one of the big five-pound notes which was the premium needed for an apprenticeship. Because an apprentice had to start his routine somewhere, the gentleman who saw me decided I should go into a big shed where, since I was supposed to be learning the electrical side of things, I began to sort out cables. There were thick cables and thin cables which were ordered either for various plant departments or for ships themselves. That was my job for something like six months. I remember the little piece of wooden board I had, something like three inches by one-and-a-half, with a number on it, not my name. One had to collect this every morning and hand it in every evening at half-past five.

After sorting cables for six months I went into a maintenance shop. This was the process. Every three or six months you changed your kind of job.

You worked either in the factory—which was much the same as any other kind of factory—or out on the boats. After about eighteen months I went onto the boats and learned where all those cables in the shed actually fitted in a boat. I was kept at this for about eighteen months.

I remember some of the boats I worked on. Some were ocean liners; a big one I recall was the *Iberia*. Some were Admiralty jobs, small frigates, destroyers, and one was an enormous aircraft carrier—the *Bulwark*. This, like other big naval vessels, came into Belfast for overhaul or repair.

All this was a marvellous experience. When you see all these great ships in the sea you probably think that they have simply been planted there. It is different when you have been able to see all the bits and pieces being made up and the end-product standing there on the slip-way. Sometimes some dignitary would come over from England to launch a notable ship, and we would all have two or three hours off to go down to the slip-way to see the ship go down into the water. The Queen's Island, more than a hundred years old, was a gigantic place where all those wonderful ships were assembled.

When I went to work in the shipyard I wasn't too much interested in the electrical work that I was trying to learn, but I came into contact with all types of different people such as boilermakers, platers, plumbers, shipwrights, joiners, welders and fitters.

One of the jobs that fascinated me when I worked on the boats was the shipwright's. He is the skilled man who lays the deck on the boat, the man who puts down those beautiful even strips that we always see on ships—strips that seem to run for miles and miles. That job always fascinated me and I could have watched shipwrights at work for hours and hours, and probably did. Bobby Braithwaite, who played for Crusaders and was in the amateur international team with me, was a shipwright. I knew him on the Island, where I also knew an electrician, Maurice Masters, who had played in the amateur international team some time before.

There were some remarkable characters among the shipyard workers. It is marvellous what a sense of humour and wit is to be found working on a big boat. There is one great big team trying to put a boat together. When you see a ship on the sea you probably don't realise how it started in a draughtsman's office and went into the shops and into the dockyard and onto the slipway, and how many different people come to complete the job there.

As I have said, I was assigned to an electrician as his apprentice. We had a labourer who did all the lackeying that was necessary. On a ship the first thing to do was to find out where the nearest riveter's fire was—the riveter had to have a fire going all the time to keep the rivets soft enough to drive into place in the ship's plating—so that we could be thereabouts around break times. It was a ritual every day in the morning, at lunch-time, and in the middle of the afternoon, to make tea.

I remember one particular day when there were at least twenty cans full of water. Some already had tea in them. They were sitting there waiting for us to collect them, when suddenly one of the shipyard managers came up. He was a man who wore a white coat and a bowler (like my grandfather's Masonic bowler), probably to distinguish him from the rest of the workers. I couldn't believe it when I saw him kick all the cans over one after the other. This was incredible, because things were rather difficult in those days and no one had much money. The reason he did this was that the cans had come to the boil five minutes too soon. It was a matter of law and order, and principle.

I used to have a special little can, with tea in one end and sugar in the other. There was just enough to make my tea in the morning, at lunch-time, and in the afternoon. I also had a little bottle of milk. When the manager acted as he did it meant that either a lot of people had to go without or that everybody shared what there was. It was a great thing that at times like this it didn't matter what your job was, or what your religion was, there was always someone to share their tea with you.

I also remember the kind of jokes that were common. One
was played on me my first day on the boats. Everybody who
works in the yard has a lunch-box, and when I reported to
the boats for the first time I was told where to put my things.
When lunch-time came I went to fetch my lunch-box but I
could not move it. The contents had been removed and a six-
inch nail had been put through the box and into a very thick
plank. Hence a great laugh all round at my expense. I found
out that this prank had been played for decades on those
going on the boats for the first time.

There was another prank played on practically everyone,
which I liked, although, or because, it was never done to me.
You could be talking to someone, and a welder would come
up behind you. If you were wearing those big steel boots he
would weld you to the deck of the ship. When you came to
move it was the funniest sight and one's reactions were
similar to those got from the old silent movies with Charlie
Chaplin and Ben Turpin.

There was a time when for a lot of people the Belfast
shipyard was one the most important places in the United
Kingdom. People who boasted of this invariably had never
worked there, but only wanted to add it to those things in
Belfast which were said to be "the biggest in the world". I
never found it this way. I always found it an effort to go
down there every day. Men went there because there was
nowhere else to go to work and because of family tradition.
My grandfather went there. My father went there. So it was
up to me to carry on the family tradition. The ritual meant
that you ended up there whether you liked it or not; that is,
if you came from the class and district I was brought up in.
Dee Street and Avon Street told you which way you should
go in more senses than one.

I could never visualise myself learning enough about the
electrical job to want to work at it for the next fifty years. I
simply couldn't look forward to half a century of going
down to the same mundane and repetitive job every day,

when I knew in my heart and in my mind that I had a special skill. This could involve me in a profession I loved. Football was really the only thing I wanted to do.

Most of the electricians I worked with were football fans—mostly Blues' or Glens' supporters—and whoever I was assigned to let me go away to Grosvenor Park for extra training when we had finished work for the day. We had a certain amount to do each day. Some days the work flowed. others were held up because we were kept waiting on other people doing their jobs. When I was able to sneak away for two or three hours the electrician I was working with would kindly chuck in my board for me—which was against the rules.

In my last twelve months in the shipyard I developed into a bad time-keeper, for I was only marking time before I went to England.

It was accepted that it was a sort of prestige to employ someone who made the headlines, or could do well for his country. While I was in the shipyard I played for the youth international team and the amateur international team. I remember going with the youth team and being allowed ten days off to play in a youth international tournament in Italy in the 1954-55 season.

I remember being in Pisa during that International Tournament and one thing I did notice as different from anything in Belfast was the "Leaning Tower". I went in that tower and found it a terrifying experience. When you are two thirds of the way up you think it is going to fall over and collapse. I suffer a little from a sense of claustrophobia to begin with, and I didn't like the "Leaning Tower". I didn't go to the top but turned back down and went outside again. That is the main thing I remember about that visit to Italy. The sense of fear for heights has remained with me throughout my life, and I can also still suffer claustrophobia in a closed-in place.

My opportunities to travel further afield increased after I

signed for Distillery. Once I played for Distillery against
West Ham in London; the reason for this game was Brian
Moore, who had been transferred to the Hammers from the
Whites. The game was part of the deal. They took me over
there to London and that was one of my first trips by
aeroplane. I found London very exciting.

One thing that stands out in my mind about those games is
the speed of Harry Hooper, who played on the right wing for
the Hammers. I have never seen anyone who so captured my
imagination. I have always been very quick myself, but he
was the fastest thing I had seen in football boots until I went
to Portsmouth and saw Jackie Henderson, the "Flying
Scot", play at outside-left.

I remember I got my first opportunity in an amateur
international match—which was against England—by
chance. There was a boy named Ray Gough who was about
the same age as myself. He was described as a "boy wonder",
and he played for Crusaders (the team that took Celtic's
place in the Irish League). He was picked for the international but had to cry off through injury and I was lucky
enough to be chosen to take his place. I played very well in
that match and, they said, gave a good account of myself. I
was chosen for the next match.

The England match took place at Bromley and their side
was a good one, including two or three players who could
hold places in English League sides. The best known of these
was Jim Lewis, whose skills at centre-forward or outside-
right were certainly appreciated by Chelsea. The Northern
Ireland team had some good players too. Bobby Braithwaite,
one of my fellow-workers from Queen's Island, and cur-
rently with Crusaders, was at outside-left. Willie Humphries,
who went to Coventry City, was on the other wing. Kevin
McGarry, from Cliftonville, was at inside-right. He was a
Catholic and had qualified as a doctor. He now lives in the
Anderstown district of Belfast, but he still maintains his
connection with football. Quite by chance—though I had

been talking about Kevin and wondering about him anxiously only a day or two before—I ran into him at Molineux. Now managing his old club, Cliftonville, Kevin had brought over a youngster, Jimmy Kelly, a Catholic, to try his luck with Wolves. On that day long ago when we played together, McGarry scored one of our two goals. Paddy Hasty, centre-forward, who was then a member of a London amateur team, scored the other with some help from me, I think.

That was in September. Four months later came a match against Wales. Hundreds of years ago Irish missionaries went to Wales and helped to establish Christianity. As footballers we were not quite without a missionary sense. At least we thought we might stir the interest of some who were not well acquainted with soccer, and we didn't think we could very easily lose to a Welsh side with so few resources. The match was played at Ebbw Vale. I have played in many parts of the world but can't remember a more bleak place than Ebbw Vale on a January day for international football! We thought we couldn't lose. But we did lose. There was a player named Phil Woosnam in the Welsh team, and he scored two goals out of the Welsh side's three. Our goal was scored by a full-back named Munster—hardly an Ulster name!

Ray Gough, by the way, came back for this match. But if he had been fit before the England match I probably would not have played at all.

Before I went to Ebbw Vale I had signed as a professional for Distillery, but the registration of the form was deferred for some days. The club knew that I wanted to play in that match and so the arrangement was not final until after the game had taken place. They put a little bit of pressure on me to sign because they heard through the grapevine that other clubs in the Irish League wanted to sign me. I was an amateur player and so, at the end of the season, I could have been free to join any club I wanted to.

I was very grateful to Distillery. They gave me many

opportunities, to travel all round Northern Ireland, to play football in different towns, to see something of the world outside Northern Ireland, and to learn how I could use my skills to belong to that world. An unwilling electrician was about to become a willing footballer.

6

"Desperate to get out"

In my last full season for the club I played in one match for a strengthened Distillery side against the famous Hibernians from Edinburgh, who at that time had the "galloping" Gordon Smith on the right wing. It turned out to be a most memorable night: I was captain and we won two-one. It was a great achievement for the Irish part-timers. Included in the line-up was the captain of Linfield, Tommy Dickson, who was known as the "Duke of Windsor" (the Linfield ground, of course, is Windsor Park). Tommy Forde, who was captain of Ards, also played. That is why it was even more memorable for me to be selected captain, with players of that calibre in our team. My position that night was centre-half. I had such a good game, it was very strongly rumoured that I might be transferred to Glasgow Rangers, or Glasgow Celtic, or even the Hibs.

Only last year I had a letter from Tommy Forde, from Australia where he emigrated. Writing of the memories that were revived by seeing something about me in the press, Tommy said, " . . .very happy memories too. I think the one that springs to mind first was the night we played Hibs at Grosvenor for the Whites, with you playing at centre-half—a most enjoyable game". I wonder if this isn't a part answer to those who ignorantly suppose that professional footballers don't "enjoy" the game. That game in particular we all found well worth while.

It's incredible how many twists my football career had

taken since Mersey Street School, but I could be playing
football in Scotland as a centre-half if the rumours of 1956
had then materialised.

By the end of the 1956-57 season I had firmly established
myself as centre-half or left-half. This was very satisfying
because I had fought to prove myself in these positions, in
which I knew that I could play my best and most consistent
football.

When I had won my place in the Distillery team things
began to happen. One time I remember I had trials with
Preston North End. The only reason I went there was
because it got me a few days out of Belfast and another trip
to England. I liked travelling very much, for it gave me a
great deal of experience and I met a lot of people. It was
probably unfair on Preston as well as myself as I was up most
of the night travelling, which meant that I could not play my
best. I played two or three games at Preston and they wanted
me to sign, but I never did. Even having the famous Tom
Finney at Preston was no inducement.

Another time I remember was one training night at
Grosvenor Park when I was called into the secretary's office.
His first words were, "You have a cold!" I said, "What do
you mean I have a cold?" "Well, you are not playing this
week in any of the teams." I looked at him showing I just did
not understand him, and then he informed me, "As far as
you are concerned, officially you have a cold. What is
happening is, on Friday night you are catching the boat over
to England again and you are going to play for Bury
Reserves." I thought this rather strange, but then he said, "If
all goes well and they are satisfied, there could be a lot of
money in it for you." I thought, "Well, I like the boat trips
and I always get my expenses." I played the match for them,
but sure enough I did not sign for Bury.

I travelled from Belfast to Heysham and not to Liverpool
whenever I went. From Heysham I then travelled to my
destination by rail. My pals around Avon Street used to like

my travels in England, for I used to tell them all about them. After all, England was a world away even though all our street names were meant to remind us that in some way or other we "belonged" to England.

At the start of the 1957-58 season when we reported back for training we had a number of injuries to key forwards. On the Thursday night, during our training session, Mr. Tadman sent for me. I knew right away what he wanted. On the Saturday we were to play Linfield in the opening game. Linfield, incidentally, had just got the famous Jackie Milburn as their player-manager. Mr. Tadman's first words were, "I want you to play . . ." Before he got his "I want you . . ." out I knew what he was after. He wanted me to play in the forward line. He knew I no longer classed myself as a forward and that I only wanted to play in the half-back line. He said to me, "I want you to do me a big favour and play in the forward line." After I blew my top, he explained that if I did play there for two or three games till the forwards were fit, I could go back to centre-half or left-half again. I went along with this because I respected him very much; but at the same time I did have my say, so we knew where we both stood.

We opened the season playing Linfield at Grosvenor Park. I had never experienced so many spectators at a league game there. Of course, the big attraction was the inclusion of Jackie Milburn in the Blues side for the first time. My position in that match was inside-left, and the game ended as a one all draw. I didn't realise how well I played until I read the *Ulster Saturday Night* where they said that there was a scout from Portsmouth called Jack Tinn (who used to wear spats and a stiff collar) watching me. Over the weekend there was a great deal of speculation about my joining Pompey or Leeds. I did not take the rumours too seriously because my name had been linked with a number of clubs from across the water during the previous two years.

I was so desperate to get out of Northern Ireland that I

could not believe it possible that I ever would--until I had actually signed the transfer papers. It happened this way. On the Wednesday following the Linfield match we played Bangor at Bangor, and Mr. Eddie Lever, the Portsmouth manager, came to the game. I played in the forward line again but my performance that night was not so good. I was so excited that I couldn't care less where I played. I can't remember the result. I must have done enough, though, to impress Mr. Lever, because he stayed over until the next Saturday to watch me play against Ards at Castlereagh Park, Newtownards.

The Ards ground is very open. It is barren place and the wind blows around all the time, even in summer. When I go back to play in Belfast in international matches we stay at Donaghadee and train at Castlereagh Park. It is always cold and always windy.

Ards at that time were very good, but our team played well and we won three—nil. My performance on that occasion was good and I was lucky enough to hit one from about twenty yards into the back of the net. I must have done enough to satisfy Eddie Lever, because within an hour of the match, after a bath, I had to go back to Belfast in a taxi with the club secretary, Fred Duke, to discuss my transfer to Portsmouth. On the way we discussed my side of the move. I was so excited, I would have agreed to anything.

Just before the Bangor match Raich Carter wanted me to sign for Leeds. The club tried to talk me into it but I wanted to think it over. It was all too rushed for me. It's like that when you are desperate to get away and there are two clubs that want you. I had all sorts of promises to go to Leeds. I would, they promised, be in the first team on the following Saturday against Blackpool if I signed right away. I told them I wanted a little time, but they weren't prepared to give me any, so it was a one horse race after that. And it was Portsmouth for me. The fee "was reported to be in the region of £4000".

I was very lucky when Eddie Lever asked me to sign. I have always been my own man and I had no one to consult, no wife to ask. I knew my father would not object and, as I had wanted for so long to get away, there was nothing to stop me. Mr. Lever informed me that I had a few days to sort things out and that I was to report in Portsmouth the next Thursday. I broke the news to my father in a pub on the Grosvenor Road. We didn't celebrate with a drink. Indeed I cannot remember ever having a drink with my father in Northern Ireland.

Eddie Lever did suggest that I could finish my apprenticeship in the Portsmouth dockyard. I told him and my father that I would, but over the weekend I thought it over and when I arrived in Portsmouth the first thing I said to him was that I had no intention of going into the dockyard. "I am," I said, "going to be a full-time professional footballer or nothing at all." I was told that there was one footballer who was serving his time in the Pompey dockyard. He was John Phillips, who played right-half in the first team.

If I had done what Mr. Lever said, it would have meant me going in the dockyard for two years. As I had just got out of one shipyard I certainly was not going into another. My mind was made up. I said no.

I have always felt that I went into the Belfast shipyard for one reason and one reason only. It was not because it was the family tradition, or that I was to follow my father, but only because I knew it would please my mother. Working in a shipyard or working in a factory, if you are not cut out for it, is like a jail sentence. In one way I hated every moment of working on the Queen's Island, although by working there I had made friends with a lot of good mates—both Catholic and Protestant—whom I would never have met if I had worked outside the shipyard.

On the Monday morning I went down to Harland and Wolff to give in my notice. This delighted me. Apparently they knew what was happening for they had read in the weekend papers that I had been transferred to Portsmouth. After clearing up one or two small things I had a big matter to attend to. I had to sell the car that I had bought six months earlier. For the record, it was a Ford Prefect. I was very proud of having my own car, since it meant that I no longer had to catch a bus to training, or walk to work, as I have described earlier on.

After disposing of the car the scene was set for the Wednesday night, when I left Belfast. Everyone wished me *bon voyage*. I said goodbye to my two closest friends. Des McGreevy was a Catholic I got to know well when I worked in the shipyard plants. He was a lathe turner by trade, but he was also a very good footballer. I played a number of games with him in the Summer League. Dessie lived at 41 Little George's Street—one of those many streets that run off York Street.

My other friend was my cousin Jim Kitchen who lived at 41 Glenvarlock Street, along the Castlereagh Road which was the way I used to go every day when I worked at the toy factory.

When the boat slowly goes out from Belfast down the river and into the Lough, where it gathers full speed, there are many things to be seen. On the right-hand side of the boat just after it starts there is a good view of the shipyard. Over the years this view has changed because Harland and Wolff have installed what may be the biggest crane in Europe (the biggest something somewhere, anyway). You are able to see this crane from miles out. On the left-hand side one goes by the Cave Hill, on the top of which is MacArt's Fort, a primitive fortification where an O'Neill was killed by the English during the suppression of the people of Ulster by the London government three and a half centuries ago. Further down the Lough on the north side is Carickfergus, where the castle was built almost exactly eight hundred years ago. It was only in 1928 that this castle ceased to be a military establishment. I remembered Carickfergus because I played football there—junior football, that is. The same goes for Larne further along. On the other side of the Lough are Holywood and Bangor, both places where Christianity was practised at a very early date. The monastery at Holywood was burned down by the Irish in the days of Queen Elizabeth I to prevent the English from using it to quarter troops. Bangor Abbey and its grounds were given to a Scotsman, James Hamilton, by James I as a reward for services rendered. He became the leader of the Scots who were sent to Ulster in those days, all of whom had to keep their property by force of arms against the attacks of those whose lands had been taken away. Beyond Bangor is Donaghadee and when you have passed the Copeland Islands off Donaghadee you feel that you have at last left Ireland behind.

In later years I became more and more aware of those landmarks but the time I first left—left for good, that is— I didn't see much. I had to go below deck to try to find the purser and to let him know that I was on board the ship.

After I found my berth and had something to eat I went to bed, but with all the excitement I found it difficult to have much sleep.

I felt like an adventurer or pioneer starting off on a new life.

ILLUSTRATIONS

1a Derek's mother

b His mother and father on their wedding day

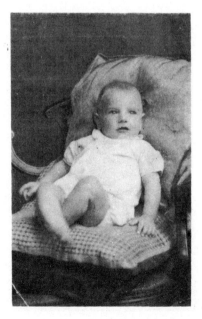

c As a baby

d At eleven months, with his older sister Pearl

2a Sandy Dougan, Derek's
grandfather

b With his father and pigeon
trophies

c As a boy

d With father, brothers and
sisters

3a   Derek outside his   *b*   East Belfast street ready
      grandfather's pigeon loft   for "The Twelth"

c   The Dougan house in Avon street, now boarded
   up

4*a* The Belfast dockyards

b At Grosvenor Park, with
Jackie Curry

c In Italy, with the
Northern Ireland Youth
Team, 1955

5*a*   Distillery Youth Team, 1957, in Belfast

b   Distillery F.C., 1956, at Grosvenor Park (with
three Catholics and seven Protestants)

6a   In a Portsmouth jersey

b   Blackburn players looking at the Wembley turf
before the Cup Final of 1960

7a Meeting Vic Crowe, the club captain, on joining
the Villa in 1961

b Failing to score in the Fifth Round Cup match,
Villa v Charlton, in 1962

8*a*　A training session at Leicester in 1966

b　Peterborough v Bournemouth, 1963; a heading duel

9*a*   Scoring for Leicester against West Ham, with
Jim Standen in goal, in May 1966

b   Injured during Leicester v Sheffield
Wednesday match, 1966

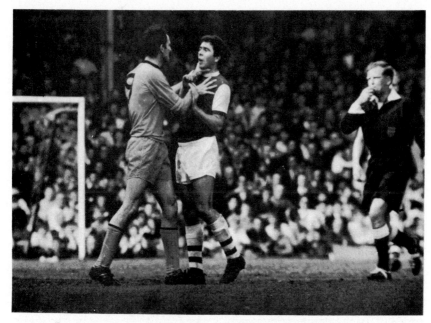

10a Things one shouldn't have done—at
Highbury, 1969

b Communicating with the Wolves crowd after
a goal

11a   Elation shared with Jim McCalliog after a
Wolves goal against West Bromwich Albion,
November 1969

b   One that didn't go in

12   The Wolves battle against
      Karl Zeiss Jena F.C. in the
      U.E.F.A. Cup, 1971-2:
      Above, in the Ernst Abbe
      Stadium, Jena; Below, at
      Molineux

13a With the Northern Ireland Amateur
International team before the game against
Wales at Ebbw Vale in 1957

b Captain of Northern
Ireland before the match
against Cyprus, in the
Nations Cup, Windsor
Park, 1971

14*a* A charity walk, for Mental
Health Research, in 1971

b Working on the book,
with Percy Young

c At Radio Birmingham, 1971

II
AWAY

7

"A very clean place"

Someone met me at Portsmouth station on behalf of the
club, and from there they took me to where I was going to
spend the next year in digs in Prince Albert Road.

My next port of call was the football ground—Fratton
Park. Eddie Lever was there and I had a brief conversation
with him. He asked me if I liked my digs. I said they were
fine, and his final words were that I should report for
training at ten o'clock the next morning.

On that Friday, because I was now full-time, I had a
cooked breakfast. Within half an hour I was training and as I
was running round the track with the Portsmouth players
the breakfast seemed to get heavier and heavier in my
stomach. Before long I was sick and this made a bad
impression. I fear the trainers may have thought I couldn't
do the running and so on. But in a way it was a good
experience to have on the first day. I don't think from that
day to this that I have ever had a cooked breakfast before
training!

I had done three years' training at Distillery as a part-timer
and I expected much of the training at Portsmouth. Training
every morning—and afternoon if you wanted to—would
make me a great player I thought. But I was soon disillusioned by the training, for the methods were far behind
those that I had known at Grosvenor Park. To make matters
worse some of the senior professionals didn't seem all that
friendly. But I was delighted that Norman Uprichard, once

an Irish (Northern Irish!) international goal-keeper who came, I think, from County Armagh originally, was there. He was a kind of safety-valve for me all the time I was at Portsmouth. It is nice to have a fellow-countryman in the same environment and in the same job when you are young; it gives you that little bit of security that you need. Norman was married to an Irish girl and he had his mother over living with him, so it was all very comforting.

I stayed in digs with a chap called Alex Stenhouse and another Irish fellow, Jimmy Clugston. At home he lived a door or two away from Ruby Murray, who made her name in England as a singer. They had a car, and that first day when I came back from the ground they were waiting for me to take me down to the sea front. It was the middle of the holiday-making season and Southsea—the resort part of Portsmouth—was very crowded. I had seen nothing like it before. The only times I had been to the sea-side, even though it was so near to Belfast, were those days when there were outings to Holywood, or Helen's Bay, or Millisle, or Bangor. Those were special days. My first day at Southsea I saw more people at the seaside than in the whole of my Belfast life. I thought it marvellous being able to have the sea-side for seven days a week and fifty-two weeks in the year.

Portsmouth is a very clean place and Reg Flewin, the assistant manager, and former centre-half, used to say that it was worth £2 a week to live there. I didn't understand what he meant until about three years later when I was transferred to Blackburn.

When Eddie Lever signed me from Distillery, my wages were eleven or thirteen pounds a week as a full-time professional player in the reserve team. When, after about six games, I got into the first team, I got a few pounds extra for each game I played. At the end of my first season I was told to report to the manager's office. On my way up the stairs I kept wondering what I had done wrong. I knocked on his door and waited; and then a voice called me in. The manager was all smiles and immediately told me that there had been a board meeting the previous day and the directors had decided to give me an increase in salary of two pounds a week. I was knocked out by this, and still am, because in my fifteen-year career in England it is the only time I have ever been given a rise without asking for it.

When I signed for Portsmouth I knew that Lord Montgomery had something to do with the Club. I was not quite sure if he was Irish or not, but after one game he walked into our dressing-room and came over to me. He told me how his family had lived in Moville, Co. Donegal, and he was clearly proud of his Irish associations. (He had, I learned later, an honorary Doctor's degree from Queen's University, Belfast, which perhaps was why he seemed so interested in the city.) I was over-awed with him speaking to me, but I was soon brought down to earth when an officer who was with him (I think he was a Colonel) said to me, "Ah, Dougan! It won't be long before we get you in the army." I quickly replied, "I don't think so, because if you put me in the Army I shall go back to Belfast." I would rather live there than go into the Army after what the Pompey players had told me about Army life. I was never keen on a regimented life, and a regimental life even less.

Having been transferred as an inside-forward after my display for Distillery against Ards, I immediately went into the Pompey reserve side in that position on the following Saturday. As Portsmouth were having problems with the centre-forward position, I was moved there and, after a few more games in the reserves, I made my league debut in October 1957, against a Manchester United side that included Duncan Edwards, Tim Coleman, and the most famous United players of that period. We surprised everyone in the country by beating them three-nil.

Within that short period of two or three months which began with my arguing with Maurice Tadman I found myself leading the attack of an English First Division team. Maybe it wasn't the best of First Division teams—but one could always hope. For me it now seemed as though I was being quite successful.

In the meantime Portsmouth had signed another Irishman (Ulsterman), Sammy Chapman, who had been a great rival of mine when he was at Templemore Avenue and I was at Mersey Street School. Templemore Avenue School, by the way, backed on to my Aunt Belle's house and my cousins Frankie and Margaret went there. To us in those days that rivalry meant as much as to other people the rivalry between, say, Eton and Harrow. We, of course, had never heard of Eton or Harrow, and I doubt whether people who went to those places ever heard of our schools in Belfast. There is a lot of ignorance about. When Sammy came to Portsmouth we put aside our old rivalry and became close friends.

At the end of October, Sammy and I went back to Belfast to play in a "B" International against Rumania. I remember that match well. Roy Rea, of Glenavon, who had played alongside me in the Amateur International team was in goal and I had the good luck to score a hat-trick. Sammy scored a goal, too, the others coming from Sammy McCrory of Southend and Jackie Scott of Grimsby. The next month I was in the game for the Northern Irish team against the British Army at Leeds. I didn't play all that well and was annoyed with myself, for I had been tipped off that if I had played well I might have led the attack in the full international side. We were beaten two-three. One memory I have of the match against the army was of the now legendary Charlie Tully. Charlie was one of the magicians of the game. Alas! he is now dead.

I was greatly disappointed that I had let myself down and missed an opportunity, particularly when the match against England, at Wembley, turned out to be a historic one. Ireland (I read this as apparently the proper title, even though it should be *Northern Ireland,* in the Football Association records) beat England three-two. This was the first *Northern-Irish,* or *Ulster,* victory in the home international series since 1927 when we won in Belfast two-nil. The Irish have made the most of this rare occasion ever since. As for me, I was sitting biting my nails before the TV set in my Portsmouth digs.

There was some consolation in the fact that I was included in the sixteen or eighteen who were picked to play against Italy in matches which led to Northern Ireland qualifying for the first time to play in the World Cup.

The match against Italy took place, but officially it didn't take place—a very Irish situation. As a matter of fact it was nothing to do with the Irish, not at the beginning anyway. Because the match officials for the day were fog-bound in London, the game had to be refereed by a local man. On this account it was declared null and void. For the record the result was a draw and the disappointment of the Windsor Park crowd turned into rioting. There was a lot of talk as to whether the Italians would come back—for a match against Spain had been called off on account of the behaviour of the crowd—and whether the fixture would be completed. A month later, however, it was peacefully concluded on the same ground. This time the home team went one better and won by two-one.

As far as Portsmouth was concerned it was a disappointing season, and we just avoided relegation. But for me personally it was a very gratifying and satisfying one, and within the space of ten months I became a full International. The end of the season came and we all had to meet in Belfast where we underwent intensive training for two weeks to prepare for the trip to Sweden. We eventually went on our way to London and from London to Sweden. I was very fortunate in the opening match in which I made my debut against Czechoslovakia at Halmstadt. We won one-nil but it was the only match in that World Cup series I played in, which seemed rather a shame. I came back from there and was the only player to play once on the winning side and not to play

again. Peter Doherty – then the team manager – pointed out
to me there and then that I had plenty of time, and that I
probably would get a permanent place in the Irish side later
on. I would have swopped all my other jerseys and all my
other honours to put on the green jersey of my country.
Whatever the game you play, if you are good enough and if
you play at top level, your ambition is to represent your
country.

There are many romantic stories concerning this. I used to
be told what happened emotionally to those who put on the
green jersey. I was told how men from the depths of the
Third and Fourth Division, men past their prime from the
Second Division, as well as some from the top of the First
Division developed ten-foot stature and showed superhuman
qualities. I used once to watch from the terraces and these
men were heroes. But within a few years I was playing
alongside them. Even if I had once thought that superhuman
bit was right, as soon as I had the green jersey on, and saw the
"heroes" quaking in their boots and not looking like super-
men at all, I came down to earth. Fantasy and imagination
often get out of proportion in Ireland, where the search for
"heroes" goes on and on and where the need for them
perhaps grows greater and greater. And the talk about "brave
little Ireland" and "its brave battle against odds" (on the
football field at least) is mostly invented by English people
with a guilty conscience.

Look at the situation regarding the selection of players for
international teams. Here in England we have Sir Alf Ramsey
(or whoever it might be) choosing twenty or so players from
English clubs and generally able to rely on them all being
available for a match. With Scotland, Wales, Northern
Ireland, and Eire, on the other hand, when sixteen players
are chosen for international duty it is more often than not
found that ten are not to be released by their English
employers. Another lot of ten is thought up. Out of this lot
four or five are non-starters. It is little wonder that when an

Irish team beats England it is thought of as a miracle.

The way English football is organised is always to the disadvantage of the Football Associations of the other home countries. These Associations are *always* "poor relations" who must beg for favours. Naturally, this is nobody's fault: things that go wrong never are anybody's "fault", but those who are at the receiving end would prefer to find out what the truth is. I wonder whether there is not some similarity between the "poor relation" bit in football and in the social and political set-up.

I am proud of the way I speak and it is a matter of pride with me to retain my "brogue". It is, of course, other people who have made me aware of having a "brogue" at all, and now most people would not want me to speak with any other.

It is often written how people who come from where I do have an "Irish charm", are able to "mix" easily, and to talk easily. Dougan, they say, has certainly been guilty of "kissing the Blarney Stone". Fine, once I would have liked to have gone to Killarney and to have seen, if not to have kissed, the Blarney Stone, but when I was small we couldn't have afforded it. In any case the Blarney Stone is *not* in the country for which I play in a green shirt. It is in another country (so they say) where to make the difference quite clear footballers also wear a green shirt. Of course the Blarney Stone, like many things Irish—whether north or south—is exploited for the benefit of foreigners, and in particular Americans.

So far as I know I can stay with the way I talk for the rest of my life. I don't think I could very easily alter it anyway, but early on I discovered the conflict between Queen's Island English and Queen's English. People in Portsmouth had their ideas about what was proper and what was not. At home on the buses I used to say, "I want a fipunny one" when I asked for a ticket. In Portsmouth that had to be translated. It sounded so much better to ask for "a fivepenny one, please". Nobody said anything in Portsmouth, but one could feel the good folks of Hampshire thinking that the ripe sounds produced by an Ulsterman were probably brought there from outer space. At home I soon found the other side of this.

I went back to play in the match against Rumania and after the game I met up with some of my friends in a Belfast dance hall. I was stopped in my tracks when out of the blue one of my former pals suddenly said, "Look at him. He's only been in England a couple of weeks (or months) and he's got an English accent." This taking the mickey out of me (or, perhaps, remarking how someone else had succeeded in literally taking the *mickey* out of me) staggered me and set me back. I didn't think I had altered and I thought my speech was just the same as it always was.

If I think back from now and analyse what happened, I suppose my friends were resentful that they couldn't get free from the Ulster situation.

I once watched many Hollywood (U.S.A.) films in which a young man from a small town goes to the big city—New York or Los Angeles—and becomes a success overnight. In those days I was the local boy who might make good. Fifteen years later I may say I am the local boy, from Avon Street, east Belfast, who in some way has made good. I have worn the green shirt many times. Being an international player means that one is a representative of one's country.

One reads in the newspaper that so-and-so is a "worthy representative" of England, Scotland, Wales, Switzerland, Nigeria, Russia, or of Ireland. Or should it be Northern Ireland? Here is the crunch. Does one in the end only play for a very small part of a country? Fifteen years ago I thought I played for Ireland. Things are different now.

8

"Some hard truths"

After the end of the 1957-58 season I went back to Belfast for two or three weeks. It didn't seem the same for me any more, for I had made a new world for myself and got a new life in the south of England. Instead of staying for a couple of months, as I had intended, I cut short my holiday in Belfast and after two or three weeks went back to the south of England.

While I was over in Belfast we had changed our Manager. Eddie Lever had got the sack, and Freddie Cox was appointed in his place. He was an ex-Arsenal player who had been in charge of Bournemouth when they had a successful run in the F.A. Cup. A few days after his appointment I received a letter from him and the Portsmouth Football Club about my writing to my landlady in Prince Albert Road and saying I wasn't going back to those digs and was looking for fresh ones. In his letter Freddie Cox said that he was annoyed and upset (and the Club was, too) because I had changed digs and hadn't asked their permission. I thought, to Hell with him and the Football Club! After all, if I was paying for my digs then I should decide where I live. Sammy Chapman, my close friend, had a similar letter because he lived in the same digs as me and proposed doing the same thing.

This was the first time that I officially "rebelled", although I did have a little bit of a say at the end of the season when Portsmouth weren't doing very well in the League and we had a number of crisis talks. I was the only teenager there who had the audacity to speak his mind in a team meeting about why the club was in the state it was in, and why the team wasn't playing well. I was surrounded by men of reputation and great experience who didn't say a word. This I felt was very strange. I never experienced this sort of thing before, because when I was with Distillery we always had team talks, and inquests, and everyone spoke his mind. After the meeting was over no one held any resentment; but at Portsmouth, unfortunately, you didn't speak unless you were spoken to.

This was never my way of doing things. From my early days at Portsmouth it seemed that anybody became a little bit of a rebel if he spoke his mind. In general terms I thought that to call me a "rebel" was unfair but at Portsmouth they held the opinion that although you had won your place in the side on merit you didn't have any right as far as tactics went to say a word, nor to offer any constructive criticism. The old saying was that in England you had to have six or seven years experience behind you before you could have anything to say.

There was no doubt that the trainers and coaches who stayed on at Portsmouth when Eddie Lever went, gave the new manager a dossier on each player. And there is no doubt that Freddie Cox was well aware of my character and reputation. I had the same argument about digs with another official of the club. He felt that the digs in which I now lived weren't in a good enough area of the town for a Portsmouth player, but I said to him: "All right, if you pay for my digs then I will go and live where you want me to live, and in what area you want me to live in." Unfortunately he declined my offer and I had to go on paying for my digs myself.

This was my first real act of rebellion. I had begun to learn some hard truths. Most managers of football clubs get to know everything that is happening, but some choose an unpleasant way of finding things out. Informers are unpleasant people anywhere and some of the least desirable are those who creep round with an ear for every private detail they might hear at the key-hole. I was innocent of all this, for nothing of the kind was possible at Distillery under Maurice Tadman.

When we reported for pre-season training in the summer of 1958, we read about our new "track-suit manager". We didn't see any signs of this except in the paper, for I never remember him changing into a track-suit. I was beginning to feel distinctly unhappy about the situation. I felt really that a noose was being put round my neck, and since I felt I couldn't express myself I got a claustrophobic feeling. This grew as I got to be less comfortable with my job. I thought I wouldn't be in the side for the opening match of the season against West Ham. I was, but I think it was on the merit that hung over from the previous season and not from anything I had so far done under the new manager.

We were beaten two-one at home and I was omitted for the next game. Unfortunately for me I twisted my ankle in the reserve match. I went over on it so badly that I thought I had broken it, but the X-rays showed that there was no break. For ten weeks I tried to get myself fit, but my ankle didn't seem to improve at all. The management and the trainers thought I was trying to pull the wool over their eyes by not responding to training and by maintaining that my ankle was sore. It was very painful and I just couldn't run properly on it. They told me that it was impossible that there was anything wrong, because a sprained ankle should have been better after six or seven weeks. I was disillusioned and upset by all of them not believing that my ankle wasn't getting better.

When I played for Distillery I never missed a game through injury, and this was the first time I had been seriously injured. Three or four more weeks passed, and I tried to make a come-back. In the meantime two things happened to me which were important and they stand out in my mind. First I bought another car; then I was forbidden to drive to the ground. I was made to walk for the good of my ankle, but what happened was that I couldn't walk the mile and a half from my digs, and I used to drive the car to within three streets of the ground. I parked it there and walked the remaining couple of hundred yards. Anyway I did try to get fit and made a come-back after about ten weeks, in a third team game. I was very fortunate that the physiotherapist at the time, Sam Bernard, was excellent at his job, and the way he used to strap my ankle up relieved a good deal of pain. I survived a third team game and a week later I went into the reserves. I believe it was a match against Leyton Orient—anyway it was in London. I played about ten minutes and then broke down again.

On the Monday they took me back to the hospital and X-rayed me again. The X-rays now showed that my ankle was broken, and had been broken all the time. When you have been nearly ten weeks trying to persuade people that there is something wrong with an ankle and no one believes you, you do not feel too good. When the specialist first said, "Oh, there is nothing wrong with your ankle because there's nothing on the X-rays," and after all those weeks the same specialist just looked at me as if I was an old horse, or an old cow, and said, "Your ankle is broken, but it didn't show up on the first plates, and it is just one of those things," I was really angry. I said, "To hell with it! It is *not* 'just one of those things'. I have been in great pain for nearly three months, and you dismiss it as 'one of those things'." I was shouting at him.

The manager and the trainer just stood with their heads near enough between their legs. If only they could have said to me, "We are sorry about this. We didn't realise your ankle was broken all the time." Anyway, they didn't bother me any more and I went into light plaster, and never played in the first team again till the following February. The whole episode filled me with despair.

It's only when you are a professional footballer that you

realise how you depend on your limbs being in good condition. With a broken ankle I had the frustration of having nothing to do all day but count the time till it would recover.

I was lucky to have a number of good pals—Sammy Chapman, Alex Stenhouse, Ivor Evans, Basil Hayward, and Norman Uprichard, to name just a few—who were always around during this depressing period. There is no worse time than when you are trying to recover from an injury, as any player will tell you.

Most days Sammy, Basil and myself would go out to lunch. Within a year we knew the best and cheapest, and homeliest, places to eat, which was where we spent most of our time. When in digs, most young lodgers have to find somewhere to eat out at lunch-time. As there was a limit to what a player earned in those days (maximum seventeen pounds per week), lunch usually cost between half-a-crown and three shillings, including a cup of tea or coffee.

The Northern Irish team had done so well recently in the quarter-finals of the World Cup of 1958 that all the players were invited back to Belfast to receive gold watches. I pleaded with Freddie Cox to let me go back to Belfast, as I was only hanging around the ground doing nothing. I thought a break, away from constant daily treatment at the ground, would do me good, and that a few days in Belfast would recharge my batteries mentally. But he would not give me permission. I never forgave him for this and it made me more than a little bitter. I rebelled at this treatment because I thought it merited rebellion.

I have always been one to stand on my own two feet; if you think you are right then you have to go all the way. In this case I knew I was right as it had turned out that there actually had been something seriously wrong with my ankle, and all the mental suffering I had gone through could not be forgotten. If they had had the courage to admit they were wrong, by saying they did not realise my ankle was so bad, things might have been different, but they did not. And then there was the mean business about Belfast to cap it all.

This was probably the start of my reputation, that grew up from my Portsmouth days, about my being a nonconformist, and a rebel who will not do as he is told. It was never my intention to buck the establishment without good reason. But when you see you are playing in a side struggling to keep in the First Division and you are in a club which is being run completely wrong, and you have no opportunity to voice an opinion, what do you do? You could talk to the captain? Our skipper was a well-known figure in the game and as a player I respected him; but I had less respect for him as a man. Because of a lack of conviction all his playing experience went for nothing because he never voiced an opinion at the right time. When I got into the Portsmouth side he never spoke to me for at least six months. I thought, "To hell with it. If I am good enough to play with, surely to God I am good enough to speak to!" We are all made differently but this doesn't usually stop communication. Unfortunately I never got on the same wave-length as him.

During the 1958 season although I was never a "loner" I was thought of as "the rebel". I always had the impression from the other players—not so much the Scots, but rather more the English—that they would have liked to do what I did. I remember another time when we were going golfing just before the Christmas of 1958. We had been told that we were all going to play, but when we arrived at the ground the trainer told us we were all going to the golf links except for one of the goalies who had to stay behind. I couldn't understand why he should be left behind, so I asked what was going on. I was told that he had not been playing very well and had let in a few goals in one of the junior sides. My immediate reaction was to wonder how twenty or so players could be told to report for golf and just one could be left out for disciplinary reasons. What petty behaviour! I quickly said; "What about the first team? They got beat on Saturday, so why don't you keep them back as well?" I was told to watch my step or I would be reported to the manager. It would not have taken much to make me rebel against this petty victimisation. From that day onwards I kept to Sammy Chapman and Basil Hayward. There were just the three of us.

It was during the period when I was incapacitated that I realised just how nice a place Portsmouth was to live in. The contrast between it and Belfast was so great that it was like living in a new world. The two places had something in common because each had a shipyard, but Portsmouth thankfully was a good deal less "religious".

One of the benefits of living in a seaside town was that, when I could not train, I would catch the bus down to the sea-front and spend the time just watching the world go by and looking out to sea.

Most mornings there were many old people to be seen, and this, in a way, was a good experience for me because it enlarged my view of life. Later on in my career I did special training in places like Southport, Blackpool, Brighton and Scarborough, in all of which I have come across many older people finding similar relaxation in a sea-side town. And here was I, a teenager, having a chance to break away from the routine of the footballer to try that of a pensioner.

Until I came to work on this book I never appreciated how much I was indebted to Alex Stenhouse for all the kindness and consideration he showed me when I had my broken ankle. He acted as my chauffeur for months, and ran me about here, there, and everywhere. Alex had been a profess-ional with one of the Dundee teams, when he was called up for his National Service. He was posted to the south of England and, as he made a good impression for one of the Army teams, he was signed on by Pompey. This was the continuation of an old tradition. In former times many Scotsmen who came south in one of the Services stayed to play football. That is how teams like Aldershot and Ports-mouth came into being. Alex stayed with Portsmouth for some years and then was transferred to Southend.

By the beginning of 1959 I was beginning to get over my injury, and I went back into the first team. I played about nine games before I was transferred to Blackburn Rovers. My first game was in fact at Ewood Park where I gave a good account of myself. Marking me that day was Ronnie Clayton, captain of the England team. I think it was that performance which brought me to Lancashire.

A few weeks later we played Newcastle at Fratton Park and were hammered five-one. Playing for Newcastle that night was a player called Bill Curry who scored a couple of goals and after the game Blackburn Rovers tried to buy him. He declined the move and they switched to me.

The normal procedure after a mid-week game is that you have the next day off. I was lying on my bed when my landlady came and woke me, telling me that there was a man from the Club to see me. I rushed downstairs and Gordon Neave who was there told me that I had to report to the ground immediately. Excitement was rushing through my body. There had been a certain amount in the national papers about me joining a London club, but when I asked him what was up he would not tell me. His only words were that I had to get round to the ground as soon as possible. When I arrived there I soon learned it was not a London club but Blackburn Rovers who were interested in me. After discussing it with all the officials and thinking the matter over for an hour or so, I decided to go to Blackburn.

I found later on that the main reason for my transfer was because Portsmouth were in financial difficulties, and that I was the only player who could fetch a substantial sum; hence my transfer to Blackburn Rovers for a fee of £12,000 or £15,000, which was three or four times what Portsmouth had paid to Distillery.

Dally Duncan, the Blackburn manager, told me to meet him on Friday morning at the Queen's Hotel. That is where everyone seemed to stay when they went down to Portsmouth. We were to travel up to London where Blackburn were playing Arsenal on Saturday and I was to make my debut. Teams from Lancashire travel down on Friday, stay over night and go to a show when they play in London. I was very impressed right away. Lancashire people have got a particular warmth and although I was a little apprehensive I felt that I was accepted right away. In the game I didn't play too well, but scored the equalising goal (I believe we drew one all). After the match I returned to Portsmouth and Dally Duncan said that I could drive up to Lancashire on Tuesday or Wednesday. He said the same thing as Eddie Lever had said almost two years previously, and gave me a number of days to clear up any outstanding obligations in Portsmouth.

I drove up to Lancashire rather than travel by train and I found this rather exciting. It was the longest trip I had ever undertaken in a car. Eventually after four or five hours I arrived in Manchester, where I got lost! I found a sign-post to Bury and Blackburn and finished up going through Bury and on to little second-class roads. What struck me in the Blackburn, Burnley, Rochdale area was the never ending miles of three and four foot high stone walls. It was very bleak. I think it was raining, and after coming from Portsmouth this was a great contrast. I thought, "What have I done?" This kept going over and over in my mind. If only I could get out of it, I thought, and I hadn't even lived there yet. Anyway, I duly reported to the club.

A couple of months before I had had great trouble with tonsilitis, not for the first time, and as soon as I got to Blackburn I started having a sore throat again. I played at home on the Saturday, and then played another three or four games, but I wasn't feeling at all well. Dally Duncan decided not to play me any more, although there were a few more games before the end of the season. He thought the transfer had been too much for me, but in the meantime they found out that I had septic tonsils. The specialist who examined me in Blackburn said he didn't know how I had played football. He said that anyone would have to struggle to walk about and do a normal job with such a throat. They took me into hospital and operated, and so far as I was concerned the season had gone.

I spent two or three weeks of the close season at home. I had decided to go home for much longer than that but, as in the previous close season, I just didn't like the environment in Belfast. I preferred the south coast of England. So I went back and spent eight weeks with Sammy Chapman and other friends before I reported back for training.

At Portsmouth we had players from England, Scotland, Wales and Northern Ireland, but at Blackburn we did one better, for we also had them from Eire. The difference between the players at Portsmouth and Blackburn was that the Blackburn players had greater ability, and more technical skill. We had Roy Vernon, the Welsh international; Brian Douglas, a real genius on the right wing; Alistair McLeod, who was a very useful outside left, even though he was never capped; Peter Dobing, who should have made a name for himself with England but never did; Matt Woods, a fine centre-half who spent eight years in the Everton reserve side and yet played some five or six years unbroken for Blackburn after he was transferred; David Whelan, a left-back who unfortunately broke a leg in the 1960 Cup Final and never recovered his form; a good solid goal-keeper, Harry Leyland; and, of course, the then captain of England, Ronnie Clayton. Mick McGrath played left-half and he was a very good player who appeared in the Eire team on numerous occasions. There were a number of promising reserve players too.

I had left a side that was struggling to keep in the First Division and went to one that staggered me with the natural ability it had. In my first full season we were lying third or fourth in the league at Christmas. After the New Year, however, we didn't have such a consistent time in the league, because of other involvements which took us through to

Wembley. There is a pattern in football so that when a club gets to the Cup Final the league performances suffer. This was the case with Blackburn Rovers anyway. Supporters thought we were concentrating too much on the Cup even though this wasn't so.

Looking back I can see there was a great waste of talent and ability. The training wasn't very well organised and this was something that made me angry. Indeed it made me feel rebellious again. I remembered how I had been a part-timer in Northern Ireland and how I thought I would benefit from full-time training as opposed to two nights a week after a day's work. But unfortunately it didn't pay off at Blackburn. Our training mainly consisted of a couple of laps round the ground. We went to a small patch of ground (it reminded me of the Avon Street "Meadow") which was called "Little Wembley"—it was used as a car park on match days—and I spent more time there than I did on the training ground. At Blackburn it was then mostly left to the players to play off the cuff and by instinct on Saturdays.

In 1956 I played in the Irish Cup Final. Four years later I played in an English Cup Final. This should be a great event in anyone's career, but it wasn't that way with me. I had been unhappy with the situation at Blackburn, particularly the way the Club was run and the way the slap-happy training was organised. A week before the Cup Final we played at Birmingham and I pulled a muscle so that I didn't think that I would be fit. I made a great effort to play in the Final, though, and I think that to declare myself fit was the only major mistake I made, in my footballing life. The team had played rather well in the matches leading up to the Final and I thought maybe it would be one of the days when the other ten players could carry me. But it turned out that the other ten didn't play all that well. We were all upset when David Whelan broke a leg in the first twenty minutes, and that made for a handicap that could not be overcome.

It was also during my time at Blackburn Rovers that I

began to be regarded generally as a rebel. It probably had something to do with my asking for a transfer on the eve of the Cup Final. One would think, "How can any player do such a thing?" I have had my leg pulled about this for ten years, and I have now given up trying to explain my motives for asking for a transfer. Playing in the Cup Final was important, but it wasn't the most important thing in my life. I wanted to be happy every day and not on one occasion in the season. Some clubs never reach a Cup Final but they can provide a good environment for their players. But the way Blackburn Rovers managed their affairs started off a ten-year decline. One manager got the sack, then another manager got the sack, and trainers got the sack as well. In the last year or two the Rovers have slipped into the Third Division and they have dismissed another couple of managers. This is the way the establishment works, and one is bound to think that the whole system needs completely overhauling. Thinking back, I am certain that the wrong people had control of the Club. At least, what they did was wrong.

The greatest problem of being a professional footballer is that spectators and everyone outside a football club take you for granted. When it comes to Saturday afternoon you are part of a circus, putting on a show. However you feel, you have to give a performance.

Until the George Eastham affair, about ten years ago, professional footballers were less than free agents. Instead of themselves doing the kicking—in a technical sense—they were too often kicked around by a lot of people who had no interest in their personal lives. Since 1961 there has been a degree of liberation.

Footballers are no different from other people in other professions. All they want are reasonable conditions and an agreed code of principles to work by. In Ireland and at Distillery I was treated with respect by everyone at the Club, including the manager. When I came to England I realised that full-time players did not enjoy the same respect there as part-time players in Ireland. There were incidents at Portsmouth and Blackburn, and when players fell out with management or with the directors, the response always was: "Well, you can't expect it and you shouldn't get it", or "You've never had it", or "You've no right to it . . .". I was always one for speaking up, particularly at team talks. As we had a lot of crises at Blackburn and as I did a fair bit of speaking up when others were unwilling to do so, my nonconformist reputation grew. Of course, being an Irishman (of whatever sort) helped it to grow. Dougan is an Irishman. An Irishman is a rebel. Therefore Dougan is a rebel. That's the way it went. Somehow it seems as though the sins of the fathers come down more heavily on some nations than on others.

Yet it was when I was at Blackburn that I saw the importance of constitutional method. When I was there I first got interested in the Professional Footballers' Association. It is only in the last four years that I have come to understand what a good job the P.F.A. has done, not only for the footballer but also for football in general.

Harry Leyland, our goal-keeper at Blackburn, was on the committee of the P.F.A. and he always told players how vital it was that they should turn up to meetings. It was at that time that the P.F.A., guided by Cliff Lloyd and their solicitor George Davies, were negotiating not only at League but also at Government level to get rid of the "maximum wage". This had long been an outstanding grievance.

The important thing about the P.F.A. is that it offers a way to air grievances and a machinery for negotiating to put grievances right. It may take time. But at least there is something that a player can do if he feels he is being unfairly treated.

As an Ulsterman abroad I can see how in my own country there never was proper machinery to attend to general grievances. There was nothing to help a citizen put a case to the authority. There is nothing sectarian about this. Catholics had and have grievances. So did Protestants. At least the ones I knew in and around Avon Street and Dee Street. I've already told how it looked there. I was lucky. I was a local boy who made good—as they say. But what about the rest?

9

"Too many have lost
the art of wandering"

There is a lot of truth in the belief that the Irishman lives on his emotions, just as there is in the contrary statement that many other people live off them. The Irishman is a kind of safety valve for the English, often doing what the Englishman would like to do but daren't because of "what people would say". I well remember when my emotions really took hold of me on the field for the first time, and what this led to. Now I realise that feelings and actions can be controlled. But it takes a long time and a lot of patience before one arrives at this.

I was pitched into the English First Division as a centre-forward and my first match was against Manchester United. Although the Portsmouth team was struggling at that period—its great successes had been a decade earlier when the championship was won twice—for a few weeks we didn't seem to be having too bad a time. But so far as I was concerned I was not at all happy that I wasn't able to score. I wasn't, I think, playing badly and the way I managed against players of great experience sometimes surprised me. But the fact was, that I was there to get the goals that were needed. No goals, no excuses, but a doubtful future. A footballer in the fierce competition of the English League is as good as his last match. His perpetual worry is that his next match may be his last.

The pressure on me was at its worst when we prepared to play the team that then was without doubt one of giants.

"The Wolves" of the 1950s had carried everything before them and had spread their fame into Europe. The match against the Wolves was important for the team and also for me personally. I was to play against the most famous centre-half ever produced by England. Billy Wright was an immortal even then, and I was pretty overwhelmed at the prospect. But I had confidence in my ability and was sure that I could do well.

When one is engaged in that kind of duel one feels perhaps something of what a gladiator in Roman times must have felt. It was me and Billy Wright, and the odds seemed to be on him. I saw it like this in advance. He was not very tall—say five foot eight—and if my wingers gave me a good enough supply I felt I could probably beat him in the air. Remember, I was a gangling six foot two. At Mersey Street I had been noticed for my speed. The idea that I was faster than most stayed with me, and I thought that my quickness off the mark would counter Billy's marvellous skill on the ground. Finally I was an unknown quantity to him. This can often be a trump card.

It is quite amazing how well promoted clubs do for a time simply because they are unknown. It takes time for other clubs to get the measure of them, but then life can be very tough. A young player of the last year or two shows this on a personal level. A boy called Trevor Francis was quite un-known when he burst into the football world with Birmingham City. At sixteen years of age he staggered the football world with his scoring feats. But teams got to know what he was like, and the fear of the unknown disappeared. Life became more difficult for a talented young player.

Well, there I was, an unknown quantity. But I would not have stayed a dark horse. I am sure that had we played Wolves again a week later I would not have been as successful as I was in the match in which I did play.

We found ourselves a goal down in the first half. It was into the second half—we were playing towards the enclosed

end of the ground where you always saw the sailors stand—
when I drifted to the right side of the pitch in the six-yard
box. I spun round Billy Wright and another Wolves defender,
worked the ball to my left foot—my "natural" one—and hit
it with everything I had. It seemed to fly past Noel Dwyer,
the Wolves goalkeeper, and then into the net. To see it nest
there was the most wonderful thing I had experienced up till
then in English football.

How I swivelled round Billy Wright was one of those
things that one does by pure instinct. When you come to
analyse it you cannot explain it. The only thing you know
for certain is that you could do it again. Presumably I simply
caught their defenders unaware. Over the weekend and on
Monday and even Tuesday I read Billy Wright describing
how I passed him. He said that I seemed to turn on a
sixpence, that for a boy who was so tall I had good balance,
and that he was very impressed with me. This was flattering.

Looking back one sees only that a match which could
have been lost was drawn. In the long run it did not make
much difference to Portsmouth or to Wolves. But something
happened to me. It got rid of a few inhibitions.

I had not scored in my previous League matches. Think
how I felt when I finally saw a goal-keeper who was not all
that used to this kind of thing, picking the ball out of the
back of the net. My immediate action was to raise my arms
above my head in what was thought to be a very non-English
manner (the English have learned a thing or two since then).
Well, what would *you* have done if you had been in my
place? There was the sheer relief of it, and this showed itself
in letting out all those pent-up feelings. What I did not then
realise was that there were all those newspaper men sitting in
the press box. Even then the media (as they are called) got to
work at the smallest hint of novelty.

This is what Desmond Hackett of the *Daily Express* had to
say:

    ... In this match of many Sputnik-high moments the

one I will always remember spotlights the new kid who
has suddenly sprung up on the sparsely populated
personality parade—19-year-old Irish lad Derek
Dougan. . .
When he scored his first-ever League goal that brought a
uranium-valued point to Portsmouth, he stood with
arms outstretched and happily let the cheers pour over
him.

Another journalist, Jack Wood, was so worried about
what he called the "arms akimbo display of histrionics" that
he went to Eddie Lever and asked him his views. Lever was
reported as saying:

It was the natural elation of a youngster scoring his first
goal for his club. He's a bit of a showman, I'll admit, but
there is nothing wrong with that.

It was, incidentally, Jack Wood's account of that match
that carried the nickname that was later to stick: "Fratton
crowd", shouted the headline, "can help 'Doog' to greatness."

Reading about oneself is an odd experience, for it is nearly
always reading about somebody who never was. This same
match produced this in the *Evening News*, under the heading
"Worrying time for England Captain":

Footballer Derek Dougan, the Irish tenor with a lilt in
his larynx, and a lyric in every movement of his cult-
ivated feet, sang happily in the bath after the match at
Fratton Park on Saturday.

Fine stuff. "Nimrod" only forgot the "Irish eyes are
smiling" bit, though he probably would have had my feet
smiling through their lyrics! He wasn't of course in our
dressing-room. I am not a tenor, and if I were, the lilt would
not be in the larynx. Does this matter? Well, it is not accurate
reporting. But the aim was somewhat apart from the game
and the one goal.

Over that week-end I read all these reports and I had an
impression that if a star had not been born, at least a
personality had emerged. That poor old Pompey were struggling, helped to give emphasis to what the writers had to say.

I was cast for the role of saviour of Pompey. I was further nominated for the task of supplying the cure for (Northern) Ireland's football worries. I read:

DOUGAN TO ANSWER BIG IRISH PROBLEM

From that moment on it seemed that everything I did on or off the field was news—certainly in Portsmouth. Here was the great difference between Irish and English football. If I played well in Ireland there were a few lines in *Ireland's Saturday Night* and that was all. In England what you do on Saturday goes on being written about, and embellished, for half a week.

Through doing well at Portsmouth I started to receive invitations to go to dances, to judge beauty competitions, to open garden fetes for charity, to open shops, and so on. I was particularly thrilled when my first fan-mail began to appear. I had never before known "star treatment", and what with the papers carrying my photograph and inviting comments from me I was taken aback. It was a change from living in the east side of Belfast.

Sometimes people said that I wasn't as funny off the football field as I was on it. I came to realise that I was two different persons—the one who was to be seen on Saturday and the one who was there the rest of the week. It's rather like a comedian who is funny on stage or on screen. When you meet him in real life he is not at all funny.

In my earlier days I was invited out to act the part of an Irishman. I was supposed to sparkle at Fratton Park and people thought that I would do the same socially. If I was meant to be the life and soul of the party I doubt whether I ever really lived up to the expectation.

Now that I am turned thirty I suppose you could say that I have reached the stage where I am mentally satisfied about most things that I do on the football field. In fact, I am like many old-timers now in that I regret reaching the point where you know—if not everything—a great deal about your game and the position in which you are trying to play. I have now collected so much experience that sometimes I haven't got the energy to fulfil my desires on the pitch, and I have to play with a great deal of strategy. I conserve much of my strength for certain bursts; for the leaps that I want to make when I try to make contact with a ball coming across; or when I am trying to outmanoeuvre my defensive opponents. I remember some of the old-timers talking about me when I was in my teens, saying what a good player I would be with a bit of experience. I thought then I had all the experience I required, but I realise now that they were quite right and quite accurate in their opinions. For then I was only a young apprentice at my job, although I was doing a job that hardened professionals of many years couldn't do. This is shown by the fact that during my time at Portsmouth they tried seven, eight, or nine players in the number nine spot.

It is only now that I am playing with real interest and real love for the game. I enjoy matches more than I did when I was younger, because I cherish them more. I tell so many young players that they build up anxiety within themselves because they haven't gone through the barriers—emotional, technical, and mental—that have taken me years to pass through. My personality, character, and reputation were determined in that match against Wolverhampton Wanderers away back in 1957. But it is only fifteen years later that I have begun to find complete fulfilment on the football field.

It is the Irishman in me, I suppose, that looks for fulfilment. There was a time when I was thought to be a wanderer. Maybe too many have lost the art of wandering. This, after all is how one finds out. This is the story in the poem by the Irish poet W.B. Yeats about "wandering Aengus". At the end he found:

> The silver apples of the moon,
> The golden apples of the sun.

I think towards the close of a varied career in football that I can understand that. It is the thought that is also uttered in these words in Michael Horovitz's splendid, unique poem, *The Wolverhampton Wanderer:*

> . . . on out over the hill
> 'that sweet golden clime' sings
> —and its echo rings—
> Hark—the Sunflower sings—

The green shirt of Ireland has one meaning; the golden shirt of Wolves another.

My second year at Blackburn was mentally very exhausting. After only a few months I realised I had moved to the wrong club. I tried to get away, but at the same time I had a sort of loyalty and I stuck it with Blackburn Rovers for a little more than two years.

When I went to Aston Villa I thought that I had at last found a club with a good atmosphere, both on and off the pitch. The second is most important, when you are involved in an emotional game like football, in which there are so many human problems, one needs to be as free as possible of such problems after the game.

When I joined Villa in July 1961 I lived with the manager, Mr. Joe Mercer and his wife, Norah, while I looked for digs. I got to know Joe very well, for he spoke my kind of language and we seemed to be on the same wave-length. Before long I was involved in a car-crash, and I didn't play another game for three whole months. But by the end of the season we were playing very well and could look forward optimistically to 1962-63. We had a good start to the season but, after Christmas, football was frozen off for weeks and weeks. During that time I got a knee injury from falling on the ice, which never properly mended, and by the time I was playing again, the team had got into a losing vein and they went on losing.

At the end of the 1962-3 season I was, I think, emotionally very vulnerable. I carried the can in the last fourteen or so League games. We were knocked out of the F.A. Cup in a match in which I didn't play. We lost in the League Cup Final. I became rather disenchanted with football altogether, and a lot of people in it. What was frustrating was to be held almost personally responsible for every disaster. Nobody ever seems to think of a team as containing eleven players!

After we had lost something like eleven games on the trot the manager was in a state of some depression. Our relationship became a bit strained. I was perhaps no more than eighty per cent fit and even so thought I had not played all that badly. So I was staggered when Joe Mercer said he was going to put me on the transfer list. As far as I can remember no other player was put on the list, so it was a kind of back-handed compliment. A footballer is only as good as his last game. And if his last game in a properly fit condition is some way out of sight then he may very well not even be as good as that. A number of players have begun to disappear from the first-class game simply because of being hurt at an inconvenient time. For a long time I resented what had happened, and held it against Joe Mercer; but time is a great healer and now I think that I admire him as much as I ever did. When one is young one concentrates on one's own problems and ignores those of other people. At the time in question Joe had problems of health about which I only found out after I had gone to Peterborough.

One of the reasons that led to my signing for Peterborough was their persistence in trying to locate me when I was in Europe on holiday. A fee was agreed with Aston Villa, without my knowledge, and they were told that they could talk to me if they could find me. After sending several telegrams they caught up with me in Munich and Jack Fairbrother, who was then the manager, asked if I would cut short my holiday and return to England. Something told me he was a fair man, so I agreed.

After discussing the possibility of going to Peterborough

with friends, most of whom advised against it, I finally signed. There were lots of rumours that other clubs, including two in the First Division, were also interested. But then there always are rumours, through press "leaks" which are sometimes, but often not, "inspired".

The general opinion when I left the First Division for the wilderness of the Third was that:

(a) I was too old

(b) I was "over the top" (how, by the way does anyone know when one is "over the top"?)

This is always the way of it when you slip down the scale. The theory is that you are "past it". Well, that was nearly ten years ago.

Unfortunately the Irish selectors subscribed to this theory and for the two years I was at Peterborough I was never selected for Northern Ireland who, at that time, were involved in the qualifying rounds of the 1966 World Cup. Hearing and reading about the Irish side going to different countries, and not being in the party, caused me a lot of heart-ache.

One day I was driving through Peterborough town centre on my way home and a headline on a bill board set my heart pumping. It read: "Irish selectors to watch Posh player". I could not stop the car quickly enough to buy a paper. But to my disappointment the player they were watching was not me but Olly Comny, who was eligible to play for Eire. While I was at Peterborough no scout from the Irish F.A. ever watched me.

At first sight Peterborough reminded me a bit of Portsmouth, although not as large. The population is about seventy or eighty thousand. There is a magnificent cathedral in the city which, like Portsmouth, is a very clean place. It was a busy place with most of the jobs concentrated in three companies, Perkins' diesel engine factory, the British Sugar Corporation, and the London Brick Company. This last employs a good deal of Italian labour and it was amazing how cosmopolitan Peterborough seemed when I lived there. It was also close to an American base which was at Huntingdon and I spent many an enjoyable evening with my Peterborough colleagues in the company of the American forces.

As soon as I had gone to Peterborough I realised that in some ways it was another wrong move. It had provided an Emergency Exit, but it gave one no chance of getting into the more important shows again. However, I was determined to be loyal to the club, at least for a twelve-month after Gordon Clarke—now chief scout with Arsenal—had taken over as manager. The year I had with him was perhaps the best of my career in English football, so far as the player-manager relationship was concerned.

In his first year as manager of Peterborough, Gordon Clarke had done a great deal, both on and off the field. He was "The Boss" in every sense of the word, and one of the few men to whom I have given that name with conviction. I always felt that I could go to his office to discuss a problem, and know that he would give his time and understanding, not to mention endless cups of tea. Nor was I the only player to experience this.

We were completely compatible with one another. I knew that he was boss, and he knew that I knew. I never tried to take any liberties with him and played as well for him as I possibly could.

As a result I found I was enjoying my football more and more. Gordon Clarke confided in me that it would only be a matter of time before I was transferred back into the First Division, and he was right. At the end of the season I signed for Leicester.

One morning I was up rather early and shaving when the 'phone rang. It was Gordon, and I was to be down at the ground in an hour's time. I never can tell this story without recapturing the emotion and the excitement. I was out of this world. I could not get to the ground quickly enough even though I still did not know who wanted me. I parked my car, almost ran to the club, and dashed to Gordon's office. He was sitting there as calm as anything and when I asked him who it was he told me it was Leicester City.

Although the season had finished there were a number of "Posh" players at the ground that morning. Everyone wished me the best of luck. I'll never forget the words Ollie Hopkins—a big, burly centre-half who had come from Barnsley: "Well, 'Doog', you're back where you belong. Good luck!" Gordon Clarke said, "It's up to you now."

On the same afternoon I was sitiing at home when a local journalist called to see me. There was an international match on the television and, trying to explain to him why I wanted to get out of the Third Division, I pointed to it. "That's what I have missed by playing in the Third Division." I never thought I would miss the First Division as much as I did.

It is practically unknown to be transferred to the Third Division and then back up into the First, and sometimes I felt a little like Floyd Patterson when he regained his title. But by the end of my first season with Leicester I was satisfied with my come-back. The second season was even better for me because I at once started scoring a lot of goals, and by November I was the leading goal-scorer in all four Divisions—with about eighteen goals. At first I didn't realise how much the crowd expected from me. The Press put a lot of mental pressure on me, by saying that I was going for the Leicester record. I can't remember who held this, but for the first time in my life I worried about scoring goals, and I went seven or eight games without scoring. I had scored twenty goals the previous year and having got more or less the same number in the first third of the current season, the coach kept asking why it was that I was not scoring. I couldn't tell him. The balls were hitting the posts or cross-bar, but not going in. Or was it that I wasn't getting the chances? What I do know is that the mental worry was considerable, and the worst of it was that one didn't know where to start tackling the problem. The easy advice, given by people who never on any account follow their own counsel, was to "stop worrying". I have already said that a footballer is as good as his last match. I could add to this, that the more a player seems to promise, to lower he can fall when he fails to deliver the goods.

Ever since coming over from Belfast my life had worked out in two-year periods. Portsmouth wanted me; then they did not want me. Next, Blackburn Rovers wanted me; then they did not want me. Then Aston Villa wanted me; then they did not want me. After that Peterborough wanted me, and wanted me to stay; but I wanted to get back to the First Division. So to Leicester City. I think I did a good job for them. Indeed, it is my opinion that I did a better job there than with any of my previous four clubs. I was bought cheaply, and in comparison with the Peterborough contract, paid cheaply. After nearly two years there, I was sold rather expensively at the club's request. I am certain one of the reasons for Leicester transferring me was that my contract was due to expire and I think I would have moved on to another club anyway. By this time the Professional Footballer's Association had independent machinery for hearing appeals over disputed contracts. As Leicester had bought me cheaply I think I could have got away to another club for a very small fee. It is my opinion now that they then wanted the fee more than they wanted the services of a centre-forward.

And so it was I joined the Wolves where I have been for the last five years. This alone suggests that it has been a happy period for me. Had it been otherwise no doubt I would have moved on yet again. It is only when you have got a long way on in football that the fact that the average player's life in the game is eight years bears in on you. My career spans fifteen years, and I know that the day of reckoning will come, that no one will want my particular skills any more, that even the crowds I have entertained over the years will transfer their affections. Maybe something will linger on.

This business of not being wanted affects people other than footballers. Actors, pianists, performing artists in general, all worry about losing touch and having to make room for someone younger. At the back of one's thoughts all the time, then, is the feeling of insecurity. It is not only a matter of financial insecurity, though that can affect a lot of people in our line, but rather more of emotional and mental insecurity. Now, when I see that I am coming to the end of my time as a player I cherish playing more than ever. That in a way makes the prospect of going both more and less sad.

The wise man who knows everything and who knows nothing might say: "You could have avoided the dread of feeling not wanted by staying in Belfast as an electrician. You could even have become an electrician in England. Anyway you would have been 'secure'." All right; I could have been an electrician from the age of sixteen to sixty-five—nearly fifty years if I had lived that long. If I had done that I would have stood still on the same spot. It is not natural for a centre-forward, certainly not an Irish centre-forward, to remain on the same spot. Half the ills of the world, not least those of Ireland, are caused by the stand-still-on-the-same-spot mentality.

10

"A man's game"

The world changes and one must change with it—or else take the consequences. There are, of course, many ways in which changes take place. And there are big worlds and little worlds. Football in itself no doubt is a little world, but what goes on in it is connected with what goes on elsewhere. I am reminded of this by what has been happening in respect of what seems to be called "physical contact".

When football was a "gentleman's game", a hundred years ago, it was a pretty tough business. The "gentlemen" went in for breaking the limbs of other "gentlemen" in a big way. There are plenty of gory accounts of the goings on in schools and universities in those days. Playing the game taught one things, they used to say, like "learning to take knocks", like "behaving like a gentleman", like "building character". There were all kinds of ways in which rough play was justified.

It is important to a footballer that he is physically fit, and this comes about partly through self-knowledge, partly through the disciplines of training. When one is young these external disciplines are useful. Later on one learns how to look after one's own fitness.

Nearly twenty years ago part-time footballers in Ulster trained two nights a week, on Tuesday and Thursday. They still have the same time-table. From 1957, when I became a full-time professional, I have had to work hard every morning of the working week and some afternoons as well. I believe that ideally everybody should have his own personal training scheme, and it was not long before I began to rebel against the programme laid down by the trainers and coach at Portsmouth. I am still sure that the kind of training, which was a test of endurance more than anything, was wrong, especially if, like me, you are tall (six foot two inches) and slight (eleven stone).

There was a time when we had to train with dumb-bells. These were so heavy that I could hardly even lift them up from the ground. I made such an effort to master them that I firmly believed that I left most of my strength on the track, instead of trying to conserve it for Saturday afternoons. I made a suggestion to one of the trainers that in my opinion I was taking too much out of myself in training—especially during the weight-lifting sessions. The reply was, "You just do as you are told; that is, the same as the rest of the players." I could not understand this at all.

When I broke into the English First Division I constantly read in the newspapers that I was a "promising player" who played well for forty-five minutes, but who faded in the second half. It seemed to be the general opinion that I lacked the strength and stamina to endure a full ninety minutes of football. In retrospect, I am certain that I did leave a lot of energy on the Fratton Park track, and that if my trainers had planned my training a little better I would have lasted the full ninety minutes without any trouble at all.

First Division football was and still is thought to be light years away from that in the Third and Fourth Divisions. There teams relied on physical force (or "physical contact"), hoping that this would make up for what they lacked in skill. There were different elements in this kind of play—late tackling, going over the top, kicking from behind, threatening gestures and language. There could be heard from time to time: "I'll break your bloody leg!" This was how the old game of Victorian amateur football, played by aristrocrats, was democratised. Anybody who doubts this can read up the career of the famous Lord Kinnaird!

Until the last few years this kind of thing was quite foreign to the First Division. But it has crept in at a remarkable rate. In my early days the teams with the greatest skill were the most consistently successful. As for the smaller fish, what they lacked in ability they made up for in guts coupled with determination, which, however, could turn too near violence. When I went to Peterborough I realised how much the physical factor mattered in the lower divisions, especially when one played away from home. In some games it was, almost literally, a battle from start to finish. But the experience of two years in the Third Division has physically stood me in good stead. I have developed a resilience which enables me to cope with physical assertion or agression. Since this experience I have not missed many games through injury received from fouls.

When the F.A. Cup comes around, you get the shock of First Division sides being knocked out by little teams. These are certainly not the result of skill, even though some people will swear they are. Most times these results come from just getting stuck in. And I mean in—just that.

It is, perhaps, a little curious that at Distillery I never experienced much in the way of physical hardness, even though there were a few who had gained "strong man" reputations across the years. Men of this type really were few and far between. It is interesting that among all the Irish players who have come across the water—and the list is a long one—I cannot think of one who is robust and made of steel. They are all ball-players with natural ability and developed skill. It is because of this that the Northern Irish team is a pleasure to play with and also to watch.

During the late 1960s the First Division became a tougher place. Some clubs looked enviously towards the cruder methods of the lower Divisions and then began to import them. All clubs reconsidered their training methods and concentrated more on building physique so that players would be tougher and better able to stand the more strains and stresses of the game. I suppose that the training we have had at Wolverhampton is as severe as anywhere, and more testing than most!

By 1971 the reputation of football was at a desperately low level. It is true that some clubs in foreign countries and some international sides had helped this slide. But much of it had come about on our own door-step. It is easy to find reasons. Often they are the wrong reasons, but even when they are right, they are not in themselves sufficient explanation. The rough play crime-rate spiral found magistrates blaming footballers for practically everything, and football authorities turning round and saying that late tackles and so on were the result of a general decline in morals. Finally the authorities of football took matters into their own hands. By a sort of cloak and dagger process, a new code was brought in overnight, so that what had been permitted one season was penalised (and sometimes harshly penalised) in the next. So began a "clean up the game" campaign. One does not criticise the new measures—because they should never have had to have been called "new"—but the method of their introduction.

It is my personal opinion that what has been done is for the good of the game. I welcome the new code for it will encourage forwards particularly to express themselves more without having to look over their shoulders to see who is behind them.

The Football League in this is like a sherriff in the "Wild West". When he sees a lot of strangers coming into town, to prevent any trouble he takes all their guns away. We have the impression that the League is trying to stop players from taking their weapons (of which gamesmanship is one) onto the field. This means that players and managers are now having to think twice. There is no doubt the measures are much tougher on defenders. There is also no doubt that a number of clubs are struggling for form because of the new code of conduct. This just proves how much some had previously relied on the physical side of the game. "Get stuck in", "Give him stick", and so on are not now as fashionable as they were.

One good thing about the way things are now is that the attacking forward can go into the best probing positions— within the opponents' eighteen-yard area—without fearing that when he is taking on the defence he is going to get it from behind. It is distracting to have to keep one eye on the ball and the other on a possible aggressive defender. I always used to worry about dubious tackling from behind. It just crept into the game and got worse and worse as so many people got away with it unchecked. Now it is good to know that one can play in games in which ball control counts for something. We can now get on with the job of entertaining the public, which is what we are there for anyway.

All of this is going to encourage more thoughtful play, and managers and coaches will have to change their ideas. I notice that now when I manoeuvre to draw people out of position I am better able to do it than used to be the case, simply because defenders have to challenge fairly, and not take me and the ball as they used to like to do. Some of them, that is. Defenders now also have to concentrate more on interception. This too makes the whole game much more interesting.

Across the years I have naturally met a great many sportsmen of different kinds. I have watched many sporting incidents on film and television. I have seen people involved in tight situations. Whenever I have asked how they have got out of these situations the answer is always the same. Pure instinct. Often people behave by instinct or intuition because they have experience of a similar situation and have learned the probable reactions. Earlier on I said something about the difficulty of coping with what is unfamiliar. Intuition I believe is what comes from a particular set of responses which are from experience, but not consciously so. There is above this the other factor: luck. I have often read of "the luck of the Irish"—but that is one sort of luck in which I don't believe.

Football is a wonderful activity for allowing freedom of expression. When that is not possible, the game becomes meaningless. It is a great pleasure to "play it off the cuff". But one needs a new kind of discipline here. Too much improvisation deceives your own side as much as the other. Think of those clever lobs or splitting passes which simply arrive at an opponent's foot or head! So one learns not only to feel one's way, but also to think it.

Players are more knowledgeable than they used to be. I am equally certain that the average spectator is also more knowledgeable. Partly this is due to the many articles about the game that are contributed by players—or by journalists out of players' thoughts. Most of all, however, it is television that has brought a keener understanding of the game. This is true in all directions. Some of the worst as well as the best has been seen, and that this is so has helped authorities in this country to make up their minds as to the kind of football they really want.

Television has won fans from many walks of life, for football, and much of that is due to the great job done by so many commentators. When you see a "set piece", you can hear it analysed. A free kick is being taken. Two players appear to be about to take it, but then at the last moment a third appears as if from nowhere and, maybe, there is a little flurry and a goal. Well, there it is. All very simple, and easy to understand. But those players have been working on that move for months, just as a pianist gains control of a difficult passage by patience and practice.

What we end up with on the screen, and what appeals to thousands who had never before been interested in football, is the flowing logic of modern football at its best. The old type "physical contact" stuff is out of date.

When you have been through many stages of football, as I

have, you see what qualities lead to fulfilment. They are, the emotional quality, the mental or intellectual quality, and the physical quality. These need to be in balance. You don't have this when you are fifteen, whatever else you may have. Nor at twenty-five. You are lucky to find the right blend of qualities when you are thirty. For me it is a matter of sadness that, while I have got as far as I can get in joining together the qualities that make for fulfilment, I am past thirty. Time for me has almost run out. When a player has got to this point—if he has stayed the course that long—he faces a dilemma.

When a man has worked in, say, the Civil Service for years and has reached retiring age at sixty-five he probably finds how much he has been looking forward to just that day. A sportsman whose livelihood is sport has this great frustration. Although life has perhaps been good to him (maybe for five years) it has to come to an end. The crux of the matter for him that life begins at thirty.

11

"International"

There is a difference between being an International and being international. There is indeed all the difference in the world. When one becomes an International—a figure, as the papers often say, on the "international scene"—one tends more often than not to become more intensively national, to think that things are better, or more important, at home, than they are abroad. We don't always stop to think that the foreigner also may feel this way. An Irishman, however, is sometimes in a special class, because he often is not to be found at home. He goes away where things are better, or where he thinks they are better.

I left home and have been a member of six football teams in England. They have given me a living that I could not have enjoyed back in Belfast, or in Ulster. They (some of them) gave me the chance to represent my country abroad. For Northern Ireland I have played in Italy, Spain, Sweden, Cyprus, Russia, Poland, Greece, Albania, and Turkey, while in Belfast I have also played against West Germany, Mexico, Turkey and Rumania. Club tours have taken me to America and Canada. So far I have not been to Australia and New Zealand (though I may have been before this book appears), nor to countries in Asia, and there are a few behind the so-called "Iron Curtain" that I haven't been to.

When I go abroad to play for Northern Ireland, or for the Wolves, the time I spend in any particular country is between two and four days. The only exceptions have been ten weeks in North America, in 1967 and 1969, and three weeks in Sweden for the World Cup. I suppose one would call these flying visits, but I am certain that I get to know more about a country in a visit of a few days than by reading half-a-dozen books about it.

In the early years I never took much interest in the countries that I visited. I was aware of the people who lived there, in a general sort of way, and sometimes one was aware of their different plights, but museums, and places that one is supposed on no account to miss seeing, have never excited me until the last five years.

Visiting the United States, in 1967, made a lot of difference. All my fantasies and all the things that I had known of since my early days, from films, television and books, came alive. The opportunity to see all that I had admired for so long was now there. This new interest was so stimulating that now I look forward to travelling more than ever, and I only regret not having taken a greater interest when I was younger.

When I was young I often lived in a fantasy world about "abroad". An awful lot of people go on living in a fantasy world, made up mostly out of travel agents' tales that don't always turn out to be true. Reality is both better and worse than fantasy but it is the only thing we have to live with, in spite of our being "made of such stuff as dreams are made on".

I suppose that most people do not pay much attention to what happens when their sporting representatives travel abroad. Of course, there are glossy pictures of tennis stars, or British Lions, or test match cricketers, to give the idea that we all live in the best of all possible worlds with milk and honey flowing all over the place.

The reality is that you leave Wolverhampton, and England, at seven o'clock in the morning and reach a destination at nine o'clock at night. It's all very rigorous and arduous, and when finally you do arrive all you want is something to eat before gratefully going to bed. Journeys of the kind I have so often to take are not at all exciting in themselves. I sometimes feel that it would be fine to go on holiday if one did not have to travel to get there.

The more I travel the clearer one fact stands out. That is that the British are very lazy when it comes to learning to speak another language. We take it for granted that in all the countries we go to, people will speak English of some sort. When problems arise, and I have known football teams held up for hours at airports, it is frustrating not to have the slightest idea of what is going on. This matter of language belongs to the "what we do at home is better than what they do" complex which has bedevilled our understanding of many problems.

When I went to North America with Wolves we went to Dallas, in Texas, to play against Dundee who were representing Dallas in a league competition organised to sell soccer to the Americans. This stood out in my mind because the coach driver stopped on the way to our hotel just opposite the building from where John F. Kennedy was shot. During the tour we also played in Washington, D.C., and while there I made the effort to go to Arlington Cemetery to see the former President's grave. These particular moments are, perhaps, the most impressive from my travels abroad.

I was impressed by Kennedy not because he was of Irish descent, nor because he had become immortal since that fatal incident in 1963, but because of the way he handled the Cuban affair and other international incidents. I was also impressed by the way he handled American affairs. He won my admiration on account of his statesman-like qualities and because he acted with great sincerity. He seemed to be aware of the plight of the under-dog in America and, with his brother Bobby, did much to enhance civil rights and to put bills through the Senate of the United States. A slogan that appeals to me is that "people matter". This slogan appealed to John Kennedy, too, I think.

I was impressed with the visits he made to different countries when he made a world tour just before his assassination. He even managed to visit the south of Ireland. He did not visit the North of Ireland, which is one of those odd things. The Republic of Ireland, or Eire, gets treated by distinguished foreigners as though it really is the whole of Ireland. I hope that my cousin Trevor McNeely keeps the Americans properly informed as to what is what.

Whether Kennedy's visit to Eire was a publicity stunt (for the Irish in Boston as well as the Irish in Ireland) I don't know. I do know quite a lot about public relations and the gimmicks that sometimes sprout out like mushrooms—and statesmen and footballers have some common ground in this respect.

I am sure of this, though: that John F. Kennedy's intention was to bring the peoples of the world together. I wonder how he would have handled recent developments in Vietnam, and how he would have handled the economic problems through which the Americans have lately been going. I wonder what he might have done about the problems that are now in Ireland, even though these problems are no direct concern of the Americans.

Russia made various impressions on me. I was much taken with the great and important buildings: Red Square, St. Basil's Cathedral, and the Kremlin, are all something quite special. But I was disappointed by the seeming coldness of the people, by the waiting we had to do at airports, by the inefficiency of hotels, and a million other irritating things.

In 1969 when we arrived in Moscow for the first time, for a game in the qualifying rounds leading up to the 1970 World Cup, we were kept waiting for nearly two hours at the airport. It was the lack of communication again that was so trying. When you have to hang around, the Moscow airport is not the most comfortable place to wait in. We kept enquiring through an elusive interpreter what the hold up was about. We were told that no one knew, and no one could find out!

The theory amongst us afterwards was that it was psychological warfare and part of their strategy. I think there is a grain of truth in this.

On this occasion we eventually did get to our hotel, though for some time this had looked to be the most unlikely outcome of whatever was going on. In 1971 we—the Northern Irish team, that is—were in Moscow again for the second time for the Nations' Cup. This time we were in and out of the airport in about twenty minutes, which was very strange in the light of what had gone on before. My own opinion was that the World Cup was more important than the Nations' Cup—hence the differences in welcome.

Our hotel was a different one this time, called the Rossia. When we got there I was astounded at its size. It is the biggest one I have ever stayed in in my life. Without question the largest in Europe, it has 6000 beds. When we arrived at Reception to check in, our party was in great spirits having got away from the airport so quickly. This feeling of satisfaction, however, was soon to leave us because we were kept waiting in the foyer for a long time. On this trip we were lucky in having a much better interpreter than before. He spoke very good English and I found out that he had spent two years working at the United Nations in New York in the translation section.

I kept asking our interpreter why we were waiting. He replied that the hotel was a very big one. Then I asked him if they weren't expecting us. He did not think this was funny at all. Well, it took an hour and a half before we found our rooms. It was all rather frustrating, but the Irish are used to frustration and the party that day was light-hearted and gay.

Our frustrations didn't end there. We lost a match which we should at least have drawn. The food wasn't good. We were kept waiting for it, and when it did arrive, it was never what we had ordered. Certain people said that this went the other way round in Belfast and that there the Russians got similar treatment. But this was one of those remarks which slipped out on the spur of the moment. I know that everybody bent over backwards to give them a good time in Belfast.

Sometimes one is filled with despair by people one meets. When we went to Russia in 1969 the British Embassy got in touch with us and they could not do enough for us. When one goes to another country it is marvellous how British people there rally round to make one's stay—even if it is only for a few days—a pleasant one. The Embassy people had a small party for us after the game in somebody's apartment, but they stressed that it was guarded by the Russians and also that it was better not to speak too loudly since the place was "bugged". In fact I was shown fearsome looking equipment in the basement for recording all that went on.

While I was in Russia during this period Pat Jennings and I had an experience, and to this day I cannot work it out. We were lying in our bedroom and it was getting on for midnight on the eve of our match with Russia in the qualifying rounds of the 1970 World Cup. We never bothered to lock our door. Suddenly a man walked into our room, and started to talk to us in German, of which I understand a few words. I tried to tell him that he was in the wrong room. After about twenty minutes I learned that he was from East Germany and was a delegate on one of those conferences that you always come across when you are staying in a hotel. He kept talking in broken English with a few German words, and he kept on and on. This had been going on for an hour, when suddenly the phone went. When I answered it a German voice started to speak to me. This was rather puzzling for how did his friend know that our uninvited guest was in our room? This is one of those imponderables that I have never been able to work out. My own theory is that it was a tactical ploy of the Russians. They knew—or thought they knew—that the Irish were great ones for "blethering" and they aimed to keep Pat and me out of bed and talking most of the night. What they didn't take into account was that the Irish lose patience quicker than some. Well, we didn't do too badly—both Pat and I have learned patience the hard way—and stuck it out for an hour. After that we told our visitor to go. He went quietly and we locked the door after him. It's still puzzling though.

Then there was the time when we went to play against Poland in Katowice in the Nations Cup in 1962. I got talking to the interpreter there. He was very friendly, as always, and perhaps a little blasé. He said that he would like the players to stay with him all the time, and to leave the social side of our stay to him. This we did. The reason was very simple. He did not want the players to drift off in ones and twos and, since all the players were his responsibility, I could see the logic of this. We always made a joke about it, suggesting that if he did not do his job satisfactorily he would be sent to Siberia, to the salt mines.

The worst country I have ever visited is Albania, where we were in the 1965-6 season. I had the impression that here there was great poverty. However, we had a funny experience when we were there, and at the time we all got a great kick out of it.

There was always a policeman on traffic duty in Tirana constantly blowing his whistle to direct the traffic. One admired the Albanian sense of discipline. We were out for a walk one day and when we stepped off the footpath the policeman pointed to us to get back onto it. We quickly did so! The policeman went back to stand in the middle of the little square, to blow his whistle, to direct the traffic. The curious thing was that there was no traffic at all. I suppose people throughout the world enjoy having authority, even if it turns out to be ineffective.

The most depressing experience for us in Albania was when we were taken to the pictures. People had been queuing for hours and hours and the officials had reserved us seats. We had to sit for two hours on the hardest seats I have ever known, watching second-rate films. Half-way through the show we all wanted to walk out, but we were told by Bertie Peacock, our manager, that this would not improve the relationship between east and west, so we stayed. The sad thing is that to the Albanians this was their big event. Why is life hell for the Albanians? I suppose it's because Albania is where it is on the map, and because it has constantly been battled over by Russians, Italians, and others. It suffers because it is a small country.

One thing about Albania is that nobody seems to speak English. It is funny how we tend to place countries in order of merit according to whether they talk to us in our language. The Scandinavians and the Germans all speak excellent English, which they start to learn at eight years of age or so. It seems to me on the other hand that Italians and Spaniards don't have too much command of English. However, I always feel that I have something in common with Italians and Spaniards. Like the Irish they are very warm races. They remind me of the Irish because they are very emotional, temperamental, sentimental, and nostalgic. When we play against these countries the games are more involved than others.

My visit to Seville a year or two ago was my first visit to that part of Spain. We stayed in a hotel which seemed to me to be one of the best I had ever seen. Seville is an old town but the hotel was super-modern. It is always this way in a poor country, that the hotels are splendid. This seems to be a case of getting priorities wrong. There are fine hotels in Spain for tourists, and for Spaniards there are cholera epidemics. But the Spaniards are hospitable and when we played there we were reminded that professional football players are given a special place of their own in the social scale. In Britain a raising of the status of some professions—not only my own—has been long overdue.

When one compares the Scandinavian and northern European countries with Spain and Italy, one realises that the main reason that English is spoken in those places is that the educational systems are better, with many more modern facilities in the schools. Here we come back to Ireland. I have always said that the so-called Irish problem is largely the result of the methods of education. In Northern Ireland surely one needs integration in the schools, not segregation. Maybe it is simpler in Spain and Italy. There they don't have Catholic-Protestant problems because there aren't really any Protestants. Totalitarian governments saw to it that deviation from the established line was discouraged. Those who went against the recognised beliefs were done away with.

The opposite of compulsion is permissiveness. One thing the Irish are united about is in disliking any kind of permissive society. We were told that Sweden was the place for permissiveness. We went to a number of towns but in places iike Malmo and Gothenburg (a thousand-year-old city which reminded me of home because of the dockyards) we saw no signs of what we were supposed to find. I suppose that if you really want something, you can usually find it anywhere. But not in Belfast or Dublin. How I remember the dullness of the Belfast Sunday, with no cinemas or dance halls open. Well, that isn't quite true. The dance halls *were* in the Catholic areas. Some Sundays I used to forsake the Puritan ways of our part of the city and go to the Catholic dances.

Travel is a wonderful education. I have been to many countries with many different systems and, as a result, have begun to learn something of how different places are governed. Having read Sir Thomas More's *Utopia* I have come to some conclusions about the way I would like to see a country run. I always feel terribly sad after I have been somewhere where people don't have the right to move about freely, to express themselves freely, to visit other countries, to change their jobs. It is bad when freedom of speech is suppressed and where when you have, for instance, worked on a book it may be censored. It is a frightening thing to be told that you may not think for yourself. It is, however, also frightening to live in a country where you cannot venture out at night and walk a couple of hundred yards, without being assaulted or molested.

When I am away, visiting or playing, I feel I cannot get back to England quickly enough. I know others who feel the same way. In England there are many problems, but in comparison to those to be found elsewhere they are small ones.

12

"Charity begins at home"

The old cliché about charity beginning at home has a great deal of truth in it. After some fifteen years of being in a kind of wilderness, I can now understand what it means. I always think that life is like a jig-saw puzzle and with every day, or week, or month, or year that passes another piece is added to it. One day my puzzle will be complete, but I don't know when.

When one travels as much as I do, one learns to note differences, especially between the rich and the poor. You can tell right away if a country is in good economic health, by the state of the roads and of the buildings, and by its modern facilities in general. Having travelled in many parts of the world, I would put only a handful of countries in this category, the U. S. A. and Canada, the Scandinavian countries, West Germany, Holland, and most other Northern European countries

Other countries, including little Ireland, may have lots of spendour for the tourists, but also may have grave economic problems. In Ireland there is very severe unemployment. When a man has no work, and nothing to look forward to, life seems quite hopeless. People become frustrated and exasperated, small quarrels become big ones, and anger and hopelessness breed a kind of madness in the community. As a nation we give aid to a lot of other countries, but in respect of Northern Ireland I am sure we could do a lot more for our own people. In short, here is a case where charity should begin at home.

I have said in this book before that I often feel that the problems that we have in Northern Ireland between Protestant and Catholic (I am now talking about ordinary folk who live there) are due to the simple fact that they are fighting for the right to have regular jobs, to have roofs over their heads, to have baths in their houses, and maybe enough money to buy a little car, or to have the opportunity to go on holiday once a year. When you come to think about it it does not seem a lot to ask for; but for many people over there these things, that are taken for granted by so many over here, can seem as far away as the man in the moon.

When you become conscious of the real facts of human existence—whatever your sympathies regarding Biafra or Nigeria, India or Pakistan, Southern Ireland or Northern Ireland, or even if you have no particular allegiance—you cannot hide away from, nor be unaware of these problems. It is always possible to take the easy way out, to pass by on the other side. I suppose the deciding time comes when you ask yourself if you are going to get involved in a situation or not. If the answer is positive, then you have to decide in which way you can involve yourself, and how you want to become involved. At this point certain obligations become clear. I have obligations to Ireland, and also to England, most of all at this time to the young.

Especially in the last five years, I have always tried to influence and to encourage young professional footballers. I advise them that they must learn to involve themselves in their local communities. If they did they would realise how much local people want them to become involved. This can be judged, of course, by the number of letters they receive concerning charitable causes. They are asked to present prizes, and to knock pennies over for the benefit of spastics. They are asked to help the sick by visiting hospitals, and by going to see mentally and physically handicapped children.

I am certain young players don't realise how much good

they can do, how much power they have. Most of them think that they are quite ordinary people, without any magic wands to weave magic spells. Yet if a well-known footballer visits a sick boy or girl in hospital, the boy or girl feels that much better. There is no doubt that some people *do* have magic wands. I have seen the results of their use. If I receive letters from people who are ill in hospital I try to go along to see them, hoping that a chat of five or ten minutes will help them to buck up.

In a few cases I have been told by doctors that such visits have done more good than they could do when patients have been beyond help. Giving a little comfort to another person makes life more worth-while. This, as we look at the bits of the jig-saw falling into their proper pattern, is what life is all about.

I understand that there is a Greek saying, that one should know oneself. I have been over here in England playing football for fifteen years, and have lived under the mental stress that one day I will be past it and no longer have the physical strength to do my work; that is, to perform for the public. It has taken me all this time to come to terms with, and get to know myself.

I am sure it is because of the places that I have travelled to, the situations I have found myself in, that I have been able to do this. I have come across many likenesses to my own way of life, and many people in similar environments, all of which has helped. But it takes time, patience, and a great deal of endurance, to get to know oneself. I keep coming back to my philosophy, with my mind being like a jig-saw puzzle, and with a little piece added each day. I suppose one could live to a ripe old age of eighty or so and then leave this world without ever having got to know or come to terms with oneself. This is a terrible thought.

In the last ten years I have come in contact with more and more children, and particularly, of course, my own two boys. It is when you continually have children before you that they remind you of a looking glass, from which you can see yourself emerge as you see habits, some good, some bad, develop. You see emotions coming out and you start comparing these with your own, and asking yourself, "Was I like that at five or eight?" There are times when children become a handful, even a great strain. They have their own problems, and if you can assist them through difficult periods of childhood I am certain that the next generation benefits. I am also certain that my kids have made me a lot more tolerant towards other people.

It is a great test when a child asks a question, for it is then that you realise that in finding answers for them you are dealing with questions for which you have been seeking answers on your own account.

I have never previously realised how great a responsibility those of us in the sporting or pop world have to the youth of today. When I say the youth of today I mean those between the ages of fourteen and twenty-five. Because they can be swayed by their heroes, there is no doubt that all these young men and girls who are in the public's eye, can do more to set kids on the right road—to persuade them that drugs are evil and do great harm to the mind and body—than many other people. I should say here that I am not a prude, nor am I so puritanical or moral (in spite of the power of an Ulster Protestant background) that I want to white-wash society.

My correspondence from the public has increased by five hundred per cent over the last five years. Boys write to me asking me to give them advice about becoming footballers. From time to time a headmaster, having trouble with a pupil who wants to become a centre-forward and who is paying too much attention to football and not enough to school work (as I once did) writes: "I am sure a word from you, Derek, would help. Could you, perhaps, drop him a line?" It often does help. When I realise my responsibility, and duty, the power that I have sometimes seems quite staggering. In a way it is also rather frightening.

Now that I am Chairman of the Professional Footballers' Association, I have additional responsibility. This is obvious when you think about it. For every time I go to a football field these days I have to realise that at times all eyes are on me. If they are not, then I think they are. So I cannot afford to be caught up in any sort of incident, and avoiding incidents is sometimes very difficult, with the pressure on players being so acute today. Looking back, I don't know how I got over the early part of my career. Now I cannot retaliate as I did in my young days. Because of the coverage of the media any act of retaliation would be on the television screen and in the press for a week or more. I would then be in a position to be shot at, and it would not be much of an advertisement for the Association if the Chairman were to be sent off and afterwards suspended. There would certainly be people who would say that he should know better. It is not even much comfort to realise that critics of this kind are themselves usually uncreative and only anxious to avoid responsibility.

I am sure that the people responsible for the new code of football conduct had no idea of the pressure that this would put on the younger players. Because the modern player is becoming younger and younger he needs a special sort of understanding. When you consider that the average age of referees on the Football League list is between thirty-five and forty, you would think that they would be sufficiently mature to cope with situations. But unfortunately they cannot always do so. You would imagine that the older generation would be able to cope with the younger, but undeniably there is a gulf between the two. This is what is now fashionably called the "generation gap". Sometimes I feel myself to be plumb in the middle of this gap. This, and the nature of my job, helps me, I think, to get to grips with the reality of the situation.

Over the last five years or so, I have become increasingly aware of the dividing line between reality and unreality, between sanity and insanity. I feel that this line is so thin and so narrow that I have been at times in an unreal world, and also an insane world. When one comes from where I come from, one is privileged—or underprivileged—in the eyes of "normal" people. So it is that I have been described on a number of occasions during my career as a "mad Irishman". When you read this and then think about it you start to wonder whether you really are mad. What people say in a loose, even jocular, manner, if it refers to your origins, can cause not only concern but real damage.

Since I have been out of Ireland for such a long time (although I go back to play for Northern Ireland and to holiday there) I can look back more objectively. I realise how for a certain time I lived in two worlds while I was there. The real world was that of my job in the shipyard and of my career with Distillery Football Club. The other world was that I saw in American films, which projected the likes of Barry Fitzgerald, the famous Irish actor with his "Ah, to be sure", his "Jasus!" and all the silly clichés about the supposed "luck of the Irish". American films made for me a fantasy world, a world of myths, not least of all about Ireland—or "Oireland" if you want it that way. In childhood, however, the unreal world of myth and fantasy had become very real in one particular. I was frightened to death of the banshees while I lived at 31 Avon Street. The rear of our house backed onto the main railway line that ran to Bangor and just beyond it was marshy land. It was just like a swamp or a bog, and the legend sprang up that the banshees were there. Especially when it was dark you could hear them make queer, eerie noises. This was one place I would not go near even in the daylight. It was most of the wee bucks who told tales about the banshees (I never remember my parents telling me about them), and this is the way folk legends are carried on. There is something rather fine and also terrifying about the banshee myth, for it really concerns the dark places of the mind and not the back of Avon Street.

The English are all the same in believing all the tales they hear about the Irish. They think that the most of them are peasants (question: what is wrong with peasants anyway?). I was continually chided about my supposed way of life after I came over to Portsmouth. I was always asked if the people back home still had cows in their houses, together with pigs and chickens. It is very hard trying to convince people who have been told legends that have come from the "Emerald Isle" that most of the folk heroes who emerged from long ago are all fantasy and belong only to an unreal world. The English believe themselves to be realists. They also have a habit of thinking that they are always right. Their idea of Ireland in general is a very strange one, but that doesn't stop them from believing that they know all there is to be known about a situation which they created in the first place. That is history, not legend; fact not fantasy.

I once believed what I was told about the banshees over beyond Avon Street. I once believed what the English told me about Ireland and its character. What I once took to be gospel truth, I find has no truth at all.

The answer to many problems lies in combining mental and physical fitness. Ideally the one cannot exist without the other, neither in the individual nor in the community. I know what it is to feel in good shape physically and I am certain that life would be that much better if facilities for encouraging physical fitness could be made available everywhere. In the east side districts of Belfast there were no facilities at all for any form of recreation, and little encouragement to take up sport at any level.

When I was at Mersey Street School all we had was an asphalt playground to play on. Otherwise we had a long way to go to Victoria Park. It was only two or three miles, which doesn't sound far, but when you have to walk every time you want somewhere to play it seems a very long way. Many people today have everything laid on, right on their own doorsteps, which results too often in laziness and indiffer-

ence to the needs of others. When one looks at under-
privileged people, in South Africa and among the coloured
people in certain parts of America, one realises that these
people are striving for the opportunity to have the same
facilities as the privileged white man. I am certain that when
the white man learns to offer to others the opportunities and
the facilities that he enjoys, the relationship between races
will be a lot better. The case is exactly the same in Northern
Ireland, except that the under-privileged are not noticeable
because of colour. They are, perhaps, only noticed by the
majority as figures in unemployment statistics.

All of this brings me to a conclusion. Although I
sympathise with every type of charity, I have officially
become involved with the Mental Health Research Fund.
This is because mental health links together everyone in the
world, the rich and the poor, the black and the white, the
physically sick and and physically healthy, but also the
mentally and the physically handicapped. I am certain that
virtually every pound that I manage to raise in Wolverhampton goes into research to see why people are mentally and
physically handicapped. Many other big charities, with vast
expenses and administrative costs, swallow up nearly all that
is raised in administrative upkeep.

It is not only people who perform in public who have
mental breakdowns, but also those who work in factories
and offices. Sometimes people turn to alcohol and other
forms of escape for relief. They too often become dead-
enders, no-hopers, with nothing to look forward to. I am
certain that if we had the machinery and enough money
these people would not be driven to resort to desperate
measures, and that they could be cured.

There is something I have found out since visiting centres
for the mentally handicapped and speaking to the parents of
such children. There was a time when parents with a
mentally ill child, or a child who is some way or other was
not normal, would keep quiet about it and not let it get

around. This was something they would want to sweep under the carpet. The ironical thing about it is that any normal healthy couple could have one of these children. It is only when you bring your problems out into the open that we can do something about them.

I am frequently asked how I first got involved with mental health research. Like most things that later turn out to be important in life it happened almost by accident soon after I had left Leicester to join Wolves.

One of my best friends in Leicester asked me if I would like to come across from Wolverhampton to attend a charity champagne supper at Lord Crawshaw's country house, Whatton House, which is in Leicestershire not far from Loughborough. This was the first time I had met a lot of people with titles and I found the social side of the evening very pleasant. When I lived in east Belfast I didn't think much about people with titles. If I thought about them at all I suppose I considered them the real "upper class", the "aristocrats", real snobs. In recent years I have met many people of this kind and found them not much different from anybody else. Some are nice; some are not nice; most of them seem well off; quite a few are not as well off as I once imagined; some live in mansions; some can't afford to live in mansions. There is nothing like finding out for oneself what people are like. Getting to know other people is also another way of getting to know oneself. With the aristocracy I discovered it was as with a book: one doesn't judge only by the cover. We all have covers.

As I said, the evening at Lord Crawshaw's was very pleasant. This went for the official speeches too. There are times when speeches at functions are deadly dull. This was not one of those times. One of the speakers, I remember, was Lady Isobel Barnett, who is well-known as a broadcaster and has also done much work for mental health. The other speakers were interesting, indeed fascinating. The secretary of the East Midlands branch of the Mental Health Research

Fund was Delia Brock, wife of my good friend George Brock
who invited me to this function—and what she told me,
added to the impact of the speeches, made a great impression
on me. I decided there and then to do something about this
great and important work, and the Brocks encouraged me.

In the car on my way home I thought of all the people
who give up time, and put themselves out, to help those who
are in need and those who have no chance in life—or so it
seems. The statistics are frightening, or at least they are
challenging. There are several hundred children born daily
who will need professional care and some form of treatment
all their lives. One person in eight is likely to have a nervous
breakdown at some time during his or her life. Millions of
working days are lost each year through mental illness. I
simply thought that if I could do a little in Wolverhampton
then the statistics might take a turn for the better, if only a
very small turn. I may say that without the response I have
had in Wolverhampton I would easily have become discouraged. In fact the response of the people in Wolverhampton
has been quite staggering. This gives one some pride in the
community.

Once again one is affected by one's own circumstances. I
have two healthy boys. I go places and see other children,
lovely children, who however are lacking in something that
makes for a proper mental and physical balance. It is a strain
to look after them. Yet there are many people who devote
themselves to this work. The least that the rest of us can do is
to support them in every way possible. The voluntary
organisations concerned with various charities are a vital part
of our society. If they did not function, the government
would be left with impossible tasks.

My interests in charity depend on what I see around me,
what in fact is on my own doorstep. All that the ordinary
citizen can do is to give some help where he can see that help
will be immediately useful.

I suppose that I have two doorsteps—one in England, but

one also in Ireland. In either case charity begins at home.

13

"None but an Ulsterman can fairly criticise Ulster"
Lynn Doyle: *Odium Theologicum*

It has been fifteen years since I came out of Ulster to live in England. In that time many other Irishmen have come out of both the north and south of Ireland and have settled in many countries throughout the world. When you think of the situation in Belfast and the whole of the north since 1969 you start to wonder why it is that among Irish settlers scattered all over the globe there is no trouble to reflect that which is there at home. Of course, an opinion that most people have of the Irish is that all they want to do is to fight; to fight over religion, and to fight over living north or south of the border. In my own mind I am certain that the general opinion is both unfair and untrue. It is true that Irishmen are fighting against one another at this time, but only in one special arena—the north of Ireland.

If we think of football we can see what happens sometimes in a Celtic-Rangers match in Glasgow. Players who are good friends, and who may play together in the national side, will find themselves feuding; not because of their own feelings, but because of tradition made apparent among the two sets of supporters. This can be made to apply to the present state of Belfast.

When I first went to Portsmouth only a handful of Irish

were living there, and three of them belonged to the Football Club. There were Norman Uprichard, Sammy Chapman, and me. The three of us came from the north and we were all Protestants. When I went to Blackburn it was different. The Club had a number of lads from the south on the staff, with names like McGrath and McEvoy, and they were Catholics. I was the only Protestant, but I cannot remember one time when there was any mention of religion, or any reference to the fact that I came from the north. We never fell out over religion, which goes to show that if you take Irishmen from north and south, and put them together *outside* their own country, they can live happily, and in peace, in a different environment. The big problem over there is not the people themselves, whether north or south of the border; it is their whole environment.

Environment is where people live in space. In Ireland it is also where they live in time. "Belfast Airport", said the air hostess; "put your watches back three hundred years."

It looks as if I have now settled in England permanently. I have come across a lot of people from the south of Ireland who, after having lived in England for two or three years, having had a regular job, having saved a few pounds, and having said they are only going to stay over here for a short time, cannot get back to southern Ireland quickly enough. I have met many English people who are looking forward to the day when they will be able to retire to Eire. I am for ever being asked if I will one day retire to the place of my birth. A number of my colleagues who are compatriots are asked the same question. I see myself earning my living from England. Many of my friends are here. My kids were born here. So I don't seem to have the same ties any more. I have asked most of my Irish colleagues if they would go back to live over there. Three years or so ago a handful of them would have said they would, because they liked the tranquillity and the peace of the old place. I posed the same question just a short time ago and the reply now was that the old place is not the

same any more, and that they don't see themselves
returning. This is very sad.

Not long ago a couple of our young players at Molineux
went back to Belfast for a couple of days break; one was a
Catholic, and the other was a Protestant. I do not have to say
that here in England they are on the best of terms with one
another. When they came back from their separate and
separated communities I asked them how it was. They had
only been away from Belfast a matter of months, and yet
they saw a difference overnight. I was told that it was like a
ghost town, where you could not go out at night, and there
was no peace at all. It is tragic that this once happy-go-lucky
town is now so full of tension, and that two young boys can
notice the difference in a very short time.

I meet people who spend their holidays in Eire every year,
and some are so in love with the place—even the people, they
say—that they are thinking about buying properties there.
One day they will retire there. They find at present that
things do not seem to have changed at all in the south of
Ireland, and they find it all so peaceful. Even during the
present troubles, after they have come back from a visit to
the south, people remark how they have not seen "any signs
of trouble" and that all is quiet. These same people, to be
truthful, are not very good at knowing what places are
where. I have to tell them that all "the action" is in the
north. Americans, I believe, sometimes like to be where "the
action" is so that they can add it to the tall travel stories they
tell at home on winter evenings.

One thing I am certain of, seeing there has been constant
unrest in the community in the north, is that the "loyal-
ists"—the diehards, the people who like to see things as they
have been for half a century persist as they were—are now
thinking twice. They are asking if it is worth it—to have the
same traditions but with the same problems. They cannot
safely go out of doors. They ask, who is going to get it next.
Maybe the last three years have been a blessing in disguise,

for these people are now beginning to ask themselves questions which should have been asked long ago. The old treasured traditions now seem to be irrelevant and unimportant.

When you think about all that has been done by the politicians of both sides, by the priests and the ministers of religion—whether Baptist, Presbyterian, or Church of Ireland, or anything else—and the Nationalists, as well as every other faction in the community, maybe it's time that we had a complete change of heart and another outlook. Then we could have a new and positive whole situation. In the last three years it seems that an abcess has been brought to the surface; indeed it has come to a head and it has burst. Now we can clear the mess, clean the wounds, and start afresh.

The situation always brings us back to priorities and social facilities. When I lived down Avon Street no one so far as I knew had a bath or running hot water in the house. There was a time when my own father went for his weekly bath to the Public Baths in Templemore Avenue. Simple things seemed to be out of the reach of all of us in those days. I gather that there has been no great change for the better in these respects, except that they have been made public. Many people believe in civil rights, and these in my view are basic rights. It may be thought that it is the Catholics who are most depressed, but there are vast numbers of Protestants with the same needs unsatisfied. Here we see how the poor Protestants and the poor Catholics of Belfast have a good case—a case which they should fight together.

Neither King William nor the Pope are going to supply adequate sanitary or educational facilities, or reduce the appalling unemployment. When you boil it all down, all that the people of Northern Ireland want is a proper environment. Nature has been good to provide a wonderful setting for the major Irish cities of north and south, but it can't be said that man has taken full advantage of such generosity.

As a boy I was a keen church-goer, and it was because of

my grandmother. She used to take me to little prayer meetings which sprang up everywhere, like mushrooms, in the climate of east Belfast. I started to become disillusioned with religion, however, when I was about fourteen, and I stopped going to church. I had always believed in the Commandment that says you should love your neighbour, but there were so many seemingly devout Protestants and Catholics who practised the opposite. This is why I became disenchanted, and I felt that if this was what religion was I didn't want any part of it. All of this made me begin to think about my environment.

The religious bodies, alas, have vested interests in Northern Ireland. It seems that they prefer to be separated and segregated rather than meet together in the way in which different churches now meet together in England and Europe. If they were willing to meet it would show they were at least willing to try to ease the situation. One can also say that the politicians have their vested interests. They do not welcome any change either.

One significant thing did happen in the winter of 1971-2. The Moderator of the Presbyterian Church of Ireland died in office. He was greatly respected by all, and at his funeral were representatives of the other religious bodies of Ireland, Catholic and Protestant, and also of the governments of the north and the south. It took the death of a man who was acknowledged to be a great leader in the Presbyterian faith to bring together, even briefly, all those different sections of the community. This ought to give people great heart, that there is a possibility for people to get together, but I am afraid that they will not get together often enough.

This reminds me of a book by Lynn Doyle. His *An Ulster Childhood* has one story in particular which applies remarkably to the present. Bear in mind that this was written before the border ever existed, and before 1920. In this passage, from "Odium Theologicum", we see what living together in the same community then meant to men of different faiths who knew friendship and tolerance.

The priesthood visited little at Protestant houses when I was a boy . . .; but old Father B— and my Cousin Joseph liked and respected each other, and the old man was a welcome guest at my cousin's house. . . . Not even a little Ulster boy could have been afraid of old Father B—. Even my aunt, when speaking of him, went so far as to say that "there was good and bad of all sorts".

. . .I was never in danger of becoming a proselyte to his faith, nor did he ever try to make one of me; but without knowing it he planted a little seed of toleration in my Ulster soul. Years after he stretched out his hand from the grave to water it.

When my Cousin Joseph died it fell to my lot to assist in sorting his papers, of which he had left a great many, being a kindly man to whom a friend's letter was a precious thing. In the corner of a wooden box I found a parcel of letters wrapped up in an old newspaper. A marked passage in the newspaper recorded a presentation to the Protestant clergyman under whom my Cousin Joseph had sat—as our Northern phrase goes. I knew him well, a genial man and a tolerant, as befitted a bosom crony of my Cousin Joseph's. I knew, too, that he had shared my cousin's like for old Father B—. I had watched the pair smoke a pipe together many an evening. So I was not greatly surprised to find among the bundle of letters—which related to the presentation—one from Father B— to my Cousin Joseph. It ran something like this:

My dear Joseph,

I hear you are getting up a presentation to my old friend, the Rev. Mr. N—. You did not ask me to contribute. I can quite well understand why, though I think, my dear Joseph, you might have known me better. But I hope you will allow me to give something towards it. For the Rev. Mr. N— is my

friend, and a man of peace, which I think every
Christian clergyman should be.*
We need a Father B— and we need a Rev. Mr. N— at this hour.

*Lynn Doyle, *An Ulster Childhood*, Duckworth 1921
(1926, 1927), pp 41-43

Epilogue

While I was working on this book my father came over to Wolverhampton from east Belfast for an important League match, in which I was taking part, against Derby County. This gave me a good opportunity to get more information about members of the Dougan and Kitchen families.

When my father told me of them all, and he did so in great detail, I suddenly realised that although they were not important in one sense they certainly were in another. For people like them are what a nation is made of. And when I thought further I remembered all the people of Ulster and Ireland whom I left behind fifteen years ago.

This stirred my own philosophy. Is it a crime to be born a Catholic? Is it a crime to be born a Protestatant? It is a crime to be born black? Is it a crime to be born white? Is it a crime to be born a Jew?

I thought these thoughts—as many others at different times—aloud. My good friend Percy immediately went to his book-shelf and showed me these words of Shakespeare in *The Merchant of Venice:*

> He hath . . .cooled my friends, heated mine enemies: and what's his reason? I am a Jew. Hath not a Jew hands, organs, dimensions, senses, affections, questions? fed with the same food, hurt with the same weapons, subject to the same diseases, heal'd by the

same means, warm'd and cool'd by the same winter and
summer, as a Christian is? If you prick us, do we not
bleed? if you tickle us, do we not laugh? If you poison
us, do we not die? and if you wrong us shall we not
revenge? if we are like you in the rest, we will resemble
you in that. If a Jew wrong a Christian, what is his
humility? revenge: if a Christian wrong a Jew, what
should his sufference be by Christian example? why,
revenge. The villainy you teach me, I will execute; and
it shall go hard but I will better the instruction.

20th January 1972

BACK HOME

14

"The football game—the final score"

There are jungles and there are jungles and, in so many ways, one wilderness is so much like another ... the wilderness of aspirations destroyed, the wilderness of not being listened to, the wilderness of working for change for good and encountering opposition, prejudice and, often, thinly disguised hatred for person and perceived motivation.

I have written about the crass open sore of sectarianism on the back streets of Northern Ireland and I have known the awful suffering inflicted upon the many by the evil few; I have known and continue to be aware of, courage and the humanity of those who have faced the wilderness of the terrorism that replaced democracy and fair play in Ulster for the greater part of the last thirty years.

What happened in Northern Ireland was a slow cancer, each week and month taking us further into the maelstrom of the awfulness: as it grew worse we developed the ways of dealing with it and surviving. That step by step increasing of the pressure by the terrorists ensured that people managed to get through, no matter what ... but if the full panoply of the terrorists' worst deeds had been unleashed we might never have managed to overcome.

I, in some ways, might have foreseen and expected the politics of the streets and the politics of the violence. I had never expected and could never have expected that those in power in sport would, like the politicians and the clergy, have sinned by their acts of omission—a failure to lead.

Such a sin is heinous in itself, in its conception, in its life and in its existence but when the act becomes one of commission—the act done—then the damage caused can be both greater and capable of containing the seeds of even further chaos.

Thus it was in the world of sport. Here was an area of recreational pursuit for the men and women of the streets where the violence where lurked. The terrible stalker of sectarianism was reaching deep into the heart of working class solidarity and, on the playing fields of Ulster, where bonds of sporting friendship could and should have been forged, men and women were hating and many of their administrators, their leaders, played on. The hearts of the people of Northern Ireland were burning and sport said. "This is not my concern." The minds of the people of Northern Ireland were being poisoned by distrust and fear and their sporting leaders said, "This is not my concern."

Here was a tide that was not being taken at its height; a tide that could have led on to greatness, was allowed for whatever reason, to ebb, and with it, the potential for progress.

In May of 1972 Northern Ireland went quiet one evening; there was a silence generated by sport. We were at Wembley and playing England; I was Captain of the team, we won the game one nil. The people of my homeland had been sitting by their radio sets glued to the game live and there was never a more quiet time in any Ulster spring since the commencement of the troubles, three years before. The great Ulster populous then stayed in to watch on television the highlights of the match later in the evening. The streets were virtually deserted. Ulster that evening was at peace and proud of an historic victory. It did my heart good to hear this from members of the security forces who like my neighbours in Avon street, enthused about our Wembley success. Most of the people who told me this news of quiet caused by sport were not from home at all, but they were English.

Back, in England, there was an alchemy that was healing and bringing Northern Ireland together. Sport, my sport, my soccer, was doing what sport should do and I knew that the possibilities were endless.

Here with the victory, the second at Wembley in living memory, much had been done. I was convinced then as I am convinced now that much more could have been done. Don't forget that these were times when sportsmen and women from all over the world were deeply concerned about coming over into Northern Ireland.

With the win in that May game at Wembley I knew instinctively that we had the power to change minds and hearts. Bombs and stories of bombs were surely doing the damage of dividing human beings, neighbours from neighbouring islands ... the English, the Welsh and the Scottish simply wouldn't come. I knew that they had to.

In the months that followed, in my capacity, as Chairman of the Professional Footballers' Association, I spoke to Sir Matt Busby, Bill Shankly, Don Revie and my Wolves manager, Bill McGarry. The invitation was clear ... I wanted them to act together to bring Manchester United, Leeds United, Liverpool and Wolverhampton Wanderers over to Belfast to play in a pre-Season Tournament in 1973.

I knew that if these great teams came a calling, they would know that Northern Ireland was safe and if it was safe for great footballing teams and the giants of English football management to visit, then it was certainly safe enough for ordinary mortals.

I don't know about you but I've always found that in times of trouble it always helps to seek and to get support. When that support comes from friends, from the expected quarter, that's all to the good.

My concept and proposal was accepted by those I

approached; they wanted to come and I have to say that at times in my words of invitation, it was a matter of convincing them that to come was a good idea and that there would be no problems on the security front. They accepted what I was saying and to add to that Sir Matt told me that he knew all would be well as he was in touch with Ireland on an almost weekly basis.

Think about it ... if there is no support at the grass roots and if Irish football north and south were not to flourish then the seed corn would be gone. Remember, just ten years earlier Manchester United came to Belfast and unearthed a raw nugget called George Best—arguably, in his time, the greatest footballer in the world.

The footballing giants recognised this and they were ready to come but tragically, the legislators and the administrators in Northern Ireland eventually pooh-poohd the idea; the reason given to me was that the timing was wrong and that the Northern Ireland of the seventies was no place for the top teams of the English game. They would not be encouraged to come and play—because of the Troubles.

For me it was a bleak and a black time. My homeland and my people were being isolated and rejected. Some from across the water were willing to come, others were not but the greatest hurt of all was that it seemed clear that there were those at home, our own people, who were prepared to build barriers and to say "NO" to the possibility of a welcome, the reason given, "The Troubles". The ordinary people of Ulster kept saying "YES" and even then in the depths of my hurt, a hurt not far from despair, I never gave up. The battle had to go on and, it seemed to me, that I was for some strange reason, the only person I knew well enough placed in the corridors of footballing power, to battle on and try ring the changes.

That battle took me to Billy Drennan, a wee man with the presence of a God. Billy Drennan was the Secretary of

the Irish Football Association and as well as being one of
the best administrators known to the mind of man. He
was also a hell of a nice individual and a decent and
influential man.

The approach was by telephone. Mr. Drennan took my
call in the Belfast offices of the I.F.A. and I was able to
offer him the best possible reason for the proposed pre-
season visit of the English teams; it had never happened
before and represented an excellent coup. Additionally, I
had sounded out Malcom Brodie, the biggest sporting
voice in the North at the time. I told Malcom of the
proposal and to say that his response was excited and
enthusiastic, would be a gross understatement. During our
conversation Malcom gave me the very peg upon which
to hang the whole idea.

Mary Peters was the Golden Girl of all of Ireland's
athletics—she had won the Gold in the Decathlon in
Munich just the year before—and now, the doyens of
Northern Ireland sport wanted to put in place at Queen's
University a new Tartan Track, and name it after our
latest and still greatest heroine.

Remember the stature of Mary, she was for Northern
Ireland quite simply The Greatest. It is seldom that great
achievers are recognised in their own life times but there
was a palpable determination that Mary's achievements
would be marked and would be marked in a way that
would ensure a continuation of sporting excellence.

Over the previous months there was an appeal in place
to raise the money for the Track. The fund raising was ten
thousand pounds short of its sixty thousand target. The
track was intended for all members of the community and
it seemed to me that a proposed football tournament
supporting the Appeal was most certainly self-justifying.

Whilst in conversation with Malcom Brodie, I asked
him if there were any other good causes in need of support.
He told me that thirty five thousand pounds was needed

for renovations and a new flood lighting system at Windsor
Park. So here then was a precise and very personal project
with which I could identify; the Windsor Park wore struck
a cord since I had played there on manys the occasion
with the Northern Ireland team and, of course, for Distillery against Linfield. I played there too as a teenager
when I enjoyed the highlight of my sporting life until
then by winning an Irish Cup medal against my beloved
Glentoran. Two projects, one for Mary, the other for
the home of Northern Ireland football—clearly excellent
reasons for the creating of the pre-season tournament
involving the English teams.

These were things I was telling Billy Drennan on the
phone. He listened intently and indicated his enthusiasm
for the proposal. Mr. Drennan suggested that we take
matters further in a few weeks time when we were to meet
up in London in advance of travelling to Cyprus to play
them in an international game.

In the meantime, he suggested, it would be helpful, to
expedite the idea of the tournament, if I put it all down in
writing so that he would have the opportunity of discussing
it with the President of the Irish Football Association, Mr.
Harry Cavan and his colleagues.

No sooner said than done and within days of sending
the proposal Johnny Giles, who at that time was playing
for Leeds United, rang me at my Wolverhampton home
and told me that his brother in law, Louie Kilcoyne would
like to come and see me in England, from his home in
Dublin. (This is the same Louie Kilcoyne who got caught
up in the FAI fiasco earlier this year) I naturally asked
Johnny, "well, what about Johnny ... why does he want
to see me?"

Johnny told me that Brazil were on a European tour
which was due to start around April time.

This still wasn't adding up but I was getting little further
information from Johnny who tried to leave matters by

saying that he would prefer that Louie, his brother in law, explain further when he visited Wolverhampton.

I disliked the idea of being left that way in the dark and I pushed for further details. I had, you see, already accepted an invitation to go to South Africa after the British Championship which involved England, Scotland and Wales at the end of the season.

Johnny went so far as to say that there was a very strong interest in playing Brazil and the people in Dublin wanted me and a few players to come down from Northern Ireland to take part in the game, if it was possible. We left it that Louie Kilcoyne would give me a ring. No sooner than the conversation had ended, the telephone rang again—it was Louie Kilcoyne. I'm convinced to this day that Louie Kilcoyne was with Johnny Giles in his Leeds home. We had a brief conversation and he arranged to come down to Wolverhampton during the week which he duly did and outlined his intentions on behalf of the people that he spoke for in Dublin—including the F.A.I.

It was during our conversation at my home in Wolverhampton that he told me of his deep involvement in football: his family had bought Shamrock Rovers football club and he went on to tell me that he was running the commercial side on behalf of his brother.

Louie spoke about the very, very strong possibility of Brazil coming to Dublin. Personally it was a statement that engendered great excitement as I envisaged the opportunity of playing against them. They were, after all, the 1970 World Cup Champions.

I explained to Louie that I had hopes for a pre-season tournament in Belfast and told him of my concern that there could be a conflict with any Brazil game. I made it clear that I was organising the tournament to encourage greater togetherness in sport, to support the Mary Peter's Track Appeal, and to gain much needed funding for the home of Northern Ireland football, Windsor Park.

We left it, very simply, that he had work to do in convincing Brazil to come to Ireland and I asked him to keep me informed. I told Louie of my impending meeting in London with Mr. Drennan and Mr. Cavan and asked if I could tell them of possibility of Brazil coming to Dublin. He said "of course."

Not long after that meeting it was soon time for the Cyprus match and, as always by tradition, the Northern Ireland squad and selectors and officials met in London. We would usually go there on a Sunday but from time to time we would meet up on the Saturday evening if we had an early flight out on Sunday morning. At our London hotel Harry Cavan and Billy Drennan and I had the opportunity to discuss the forthcoming tournament to be held in Belfast in late July 1973. We did so and were making good progress ... all the time my mind kept returning to the excitement of a possible contest against Brazil—a dream come true if you like. This was indeed a dream and a dream not only for the players but for the sporting fraternity throughout the island of Ireland. Here would be a first and I was about to break the news of the idea, for the first time, to the bosses of Irish soccer. The suggestion was that there should be a number of players coming together, from North and South, to play in such a unique game.

I was excited about the All-Ireland idea, and why wouldn't I be ... this would be the greatest sporting opportunity of my life and the same would apply to all of my colleagues. The excitement in my voice and my body language was palpable. ... Here I was in small room in a London hotel. There were three of us present. Harry Cavan and Billy Drennan listened to what I was saying ... the English wanted to come and they would ... the great pre-season tournament could go ahead ... urgently needed funds for the track and for Windsor Park would be raised ... Northern Ireland would be brought in from the cold because she would have yet again, in the midst of her troubles, the support and the confidence of her friends ... the footballing giants of England.

All I had to do, subject to the IFA's endorsement was to contact Messrs Busby, Shankly, Revie and McGarry and tell them that all was agreed.

Harry Cavan was slightly to the right of being luke warm in his response to the English teams coming over here for the tournament. Billy Drennan was more than affable and indicated that he wanted the tournament to go ahead. Mr. Drennan, and I say it again, was both a gentleman and a far sighted professional administrator.

And there was more, there was more—as Jimmy Cricket would say—there was indeed more and I was outside myself with the excitement of the story I was about to tell.

Here I was laying out my shop window for progress in front of the two top men of Ulster soccer ... and the prize, the greatest prize of all perhaps, was that we might bring Brazil to Dublin and play them with a team that had never before graced the playing fields of the island ... an All-Ireland team against the world champions, perhaps the finest team in the history of football.

You might well imagine my expectation of great enthusiasm in the response. It was a bit like taking a penalty kick in the last moments of a drawn cup final ... there was excitement in the air and I feel to this day that if a machine existed for measuring excitement and if it had been there on that evening ... the needle would have gone off the Richter Scale.

My hands were wet with the sweat of the nervous tension. Here, I thought, we were talking about history in the making ... here we were talking about leadership ... here we were talking about building bridges ... here we were talking about friendship, trust and building a new world for the future.

Then came the moment that I will remember for the rest of my life. I felt that the news that I had just brought was received like a bombshell by the President, Mr. Cavan.

Here in the face of what was for me a great moment in my footballing life, I was confronted by a cold and stoney silence. For me, the idea of the All Ireland team created the possibility of contributing to the healing of divisions, perhaps ... certainly people would come together and in a society in which neighbours were rent apart by the bigatory and hate of the Irish situation, a temporary sporting unity would be a major achievement.

The response of Harry Cavan to the news I brought was precise and well focused. He informed me, tersely, that he would put the discussions to members of the Irish Football Association: Mr. Drennan warmly told me he would be in touch and would let me know what was happening. When we met in London that evening I was Captain of the Northern Ireland team and had been for four years.

We went to Cyprus, played the game, came home and went out separate ways but the issues raised that night in the hotel have never been discussed again to this day. Neither man came back to me.

After that night, I was never selected again to play for my country. Our time span in that small London hotel room was barely thirty minutes.

Some time later I was taking part in a television programme at the Sporting Club at Molineux, the home of Wolverhampton Wanderers Football Club. Also taking part was Sir Stanley Rous, President of F.I.F.A.

During the social side of the evening Sir Stanley turned to me and took me by surprise when he asked: "Dougan," that was the way he addressed all footballers, "what have you done to upset my Vice-President Harry Cavan?"

I said, "what do you mean Sir Stanley?"

He went on to tell me that Harry Cavan tried to use "every trick in the book" to get the Brazil match with the

All-Ireland team, stopped, cancelled, aborted, wiped of the very face of the earth itself.

I was speechless and then it made so much sense.

I wondered just why Sir Stanley had formed the opinion that I had "upset"—his word—Mr. Harry Cavan. I certainly hadn't realised that there had or could have been any upset. There was no reason for it and I simply was a loss for words but not for thoughts.

The pieces on the board came together and I knew immediately that the man at the top of Northern Ireland Soccer had tried to obstruct the possible progress of trust and togetherness.

Rous went on to tell me that he had made it clear to Harry Cavan that he as President of F.I.F.A. didn't have the right or the authority, or the wish the cancel the Brazil game.

Mr. Cavan was not beaten in his crusade ... "Security" that was the cry that he used to try and get his way.

And in the use of "security" as the means of stopping the game there was a great irony ... here we had footballers from across the water plus Busby, Shankly, Revie, McGarry their managers, all willing to come across for the Tournament—security for them was not an issue.

Security was never an issue for the thousands of fans who were traversing the battle lines of Ulster ever Saturday to support their teams in almost every sport.

Security only became an issue in the mind of a man who for some strange and unexplained reason could not bring himself to support a concept which could have been the harbinger of better things to come: a development, a moment of conception if you like for the much needed infant of trust between peoples in Ireland. Security that was never an issue for those who cared was being used as an excuse to prevent a happening which could have led to a time when bombs and bullets and bigatory and mistrust and, "security" would have been no more.

But in the end Harry Cavan half got his way. The Brazilians agreed and the game would be played but the All-Ireland Eleven couldn't be called that. Harry Cavan had worked tirelessly to prevent the use of the name and he succeeded ... We were forced to drop the name All-Ireland Eleven and had to accept the honourable replacement title. A Shamrock Rovers Select Eleven.

This is what I wrote after that historic day and before the Stanley Rous conversation.

"They didn't say it couldn't be done. They said it shouldn't be done. It was done and afterwards they couldn't find any fault with it, so they said nothing."

It sounds like a conundrum ... it was the All-Ireland football match against Brazil, in a rugby stadium in Dublin, on the 3rd July 1973.

They were those who were opposed to the match, who even at the last moment tried to get it called off, raising such bogies as:

Security:

Reservations of some clubs over releasing players.

I have to admit that security was a problem ... how to stop the crowds of excited fans swarming onto the pitch at the end to cheer and shout their acclaim because they appreciated the gesture by the Northerners coming down irrespective of possible repercussions. But there were no bombs ... almost thirty five thousand people had a day to remember.

Is that to be the end of it—a day to remember? It ought to have been a prelude to a United Ireland football team. What was proved that day at Lansdowne Road was not only could great sporting events be held without security problems but that an All Ireland side is a practical proposition.

As one of the selectors I have to admit I had a few anxious moments during the game, when we were four one down after sixty one minutes! I could imagine the gleefully

malicious smiles of those who had set their faces against a
united team. If we took a hammering, they could hide any
political motives in their rejection of the idea and argue
that in straight forward footballing terms it did not make
sense. To have failed at this initial exploratory moment
would have been to have played right into their hands.
They surely would have said that all the match showed
was the ability of an All-Ireland side to be well and truly
beaten by an established international team.

But back came the Shamrock Rovers (All-Ireland
Eleven) to reduce the margin 4–3.

The sports headlines next day testified to the impact ...
"All-Ireland Eleven Show What Can Be Achieved."

"So Fabulous ... Now Let's Stick Together!"
"Irish are United—World Champs Get a Fright."
"Brazilians Rocked by United Irishmen."

It is not for me to try to interpret such headlines as political
slogans and nor would I want to. I'm talking here about
sporting excellence and the bringing of people together
through our sport, the great game of soccer.

It would be grossly misleading and tendentious to capi-
talise on them in a political sense. I have no axe to grind
on the Blarney Stone and am not arguing the case for or
against a political United Ireland. All I want to argue is
that there is a need for an All-Ireland football team to do
competitively what, against Brazil, we proved possible.

It makes so much sense to combine in Rugby, Boxing,
Hockey, Cricket and Swimming while remaining polarised
in the game of soccer ... North goes North, and South
goes South and never the twain shall meet!

There is no doubt whatsoever that vested political interest in soccer are at the root of the problem. It is also
likely that a number of officials in the respective football
associations North and South are anxious to preserve their
autonomy and thus their power. Having said that I recall

well that in the moments, hours and days after the Brazil
game, the men in charge, those at the top, gave me the
clear impression that they would be glad to surrender their
power in the interest of an All Ireland Association. Such
coming together would make available players of the ilk
of Giles, Conroy, Givens, Mulligan, Martin, Heighway ...
etc. Here would be a base of power for competition in the
world arena.

Remember what we did against Brazil ... we almost
beat them ... what an achievement and remember too we
were short of good and important players because of
holidays and injuries.

What I'm saying here is no longer a vague theory, it is
a reality with purpose and with meaning ... we trailblazed;
the historical notion was put to the test at Lansdowne
Road on that July day. The result of our best endeavours
must surely be that no one can be left in any doubt about
what I consider to be a clear and simple fact—the time
has come to establish an All Ireland team.

As it turned out we got the best of two, or should I say
three worlds—the world to the North, the world to the
South, and, of course, the world beyond our shores, the
world of Brazil then the greatest side on earth.

I was very apprehensive when I approached my col-
leagues in the North wondering if they would go along
with me and trust me. I was, for the first time in their
sporting lives, asking them to join an All-Ireland team and
I wondered, just briefly wondered, how they would react.
My concerns were without foundation because they all—
Pat Jennings, David Craig, Alan Hunter, Martin O'Neill,
Liam O'Kane, Brian Hamilton—they all grabbed the
chance and joined me on the field in Dublin against the
World Champions.

Here was our greatest moment and for me the end of
the international road. That road had taken me from the
award of a gold watch recognising my presence in the 1958

World Cup Team ... that elegant time piece is for my eldest son. A.D. Dougan, named after me.

That road ended just seven games before the occasion of a second gold presentation, what would and could have been my 50th appearance for my country ... that watch, the one that never came, would have been for my second son Nicholas.

Now you might well believe that these are the smallest of considerations and are of little importance but in the world of struggle and sport and in the heat of the battle sometimes even the smallest and most personal of things can cut deeply and sorely wound.

But everything has its price and mine was being made a citizen of the coldlands of isolation and exclusion. The price was paid and still, to this day, the final reward for the people who play and who follow our great sport of soccer has not been gained. The will remains in the hearts of many and maybe, just maybe, the right time will come.

I'm often asked about the future. I pause. The future? In the words of Mort Sahl,

"The Future. It Lies Ahead."

Footnote:

I always said that when Pat Jennings retired that event would mark the end of Northern Ireland's prospects for international success in the European and World Cup Competitions. Pat retired after the tournament in Mexico in the summer of 1986 and at the time was the world record holder with one hundred and nineteen caps. Pat Jennings was the last of the truly greats to wear the green of Northern Ireland.

I said that this occasion would be the start of the demise, the beginning of the end. I think that I can be proved to have been right.

A couple of years later Gerry Kelly of Ulster Television invited me to come onto his show Kelly at Large. On the programme that evening was the world boxing champion Barry McGuigan and Ireland's favourite son, George Best. My involvement with this outstanding sporting pair was to take part in a discussion about the concept of an All Ireland football team. I felt at the end of the programme it had been slightly unbalanced as the selected audience were more against than for the idea. The audience was not balanced. After the programme I could not walk away from a discussion with a number of Linfield/Glasgow Rangers supporters whose main thrust was that the south only wanted to join forces with them because of Northern Ireland's World Cup success in 1982 in Spain and the '86 tournament in Brazil. I must admit that I did very much ponder what they were saying but not for long for they were talking with their hearts and not their heads. Think of the time scale, it was a year before the appointment of Jack Charlton and I think Jack's ten years are carved in tablets of stone as they have been simply fantastic under circumstances of limited resources both human and financial.

I am the first to recognise that for a nation of five million people to have qualified for four consecutive World Cups starting in 1982 and considering the fierce competition, is simply unbelievable. But in the getting there to the final stages of the most prestigious tournament on this earth, expectations of the teams were running high, they were at their highest, and much was being demanded. The cult of Irish Soccer Heroism was well and truly born and the greatest hero of the pack was Jack. Even Jack Charlton with the touch of Midas could not produce the miracle of goals, desperately needed to get Ireland beyond the quarter final stages, just like his predecessors in Northern Ireland. Billy Bingham, and the late Peter Doherty.

15

"Hatred ... where does it come from?"

I have thought about those words so much. For years the consequences of hatred have surrounded me. The suffering that people cause to people and all the while no one willing to bring it to an end.

Take the game I love, Soccer. I have played football in every country in Europe, South Africa, The Middle East, South America, North America, New Zealand and Australia. Good players were plenty and so were the teams. I played against many of them during the course of a very long career.

Consider ... the average life of a footballer is eight years but I was fortunate in spite of some appalling injuries ... those injuries, on and off the pitch took a good two years out of my soccer life ... but, as things go, I was extremely lucky.

Footballing and deep searing anger are in my experience poles apart, mutually exclusive if you like ... there is from time to time the anger and the violence of the terraces but that's mostly down to football tribalism or, in so many cases, a badness that often finds expression within the security of the crowds on the terraces.

I remember well coming across that kind of anger and hatred when I played in Turkey for Northern Ireland and, while playing for Wolves against Lazio in Rome. It was the anger of the football pitch and of the spectators on the terraces and, in a kind of way, it was expected and therefore, while unacceptable, it was in a kind of a way understandable.

In Turkey it wasn't the players but the problems lay with the spectators. It was a tough game, one of the most difficult I have ever known. It was a physical contest that demanded responses from me on the field. Those responses included challenging the goalkeeper within the rules of the game, but saying that, he sometimes ended up in the back of the net. Necessarily I took on the defenders in what came close at times to what might be regarded as the hand to hand fighting of the turf. These were tough times, this was the toughest of games.

Turkey were playing badly—we eventually won three nil—and the reaction from the terraces to their inept performance and the battles on the field was the abuse and potential for violence that literally echoed around the ground.

At half-time the venom spilled over and engulfed the entire arena in Ankara ... we felt it as players and we were concerned for our well being; the spectators were creating it, the security (an armed presence of police) knew too what was happening and were filled with fear that developments would get out of control.

I never experienced anything like it in my life up to then. The stadium was mad with the angry beating of drums, roars of hatred from the stands and the terraces ... there was spitting in the way of the frothing mouth of a rabid dog and the hands of those who watched our efforts on the field of play turned into claws that tried to tear down the fencing that surrounded us and kept us safe.

It was then at half-time that my personal security came into sharp focus; two armed soldiers, part of the security operation, came and stood by me side-by-side, and escorted me from the field of play and into the relative safety of the dressing room. They stayed with me, I was a prisoner for my own safety and for Billy Bingham it was a managerial challenge he had never before encountered. Billy was, to put it in the Ulster way, gob-smacked. He managed nevertheless to get through his team talk. Billy knew that night that what was happening was serious, very serious indeed, and in his own quiet way was, like the security forces, unsure of what would happen next. Fortunately the second half for the crowd was an anti-climax because their team failed to rise to the occasion, their performance continued to deteriorate and we eventually ran over them. The level of our dominance succeeded in quelling the anger and the hatred ... in so many ways the spectators rejected their team, lost interest and were no longer wanting to fight and kill.

To me the game against Turkey was a frightening episode but the match against Lazio in Rome was the most violent on the pitch that I ever encountered in more than a thousand football matches. Here with a fight to the death and it felt like it. Rome was the right setting and from the first whistle blowing the Lazio players were hell bent on maiming some of our players. Wolves had never seen anything like it; the level of hatred had spilled over from the first game at Molineux in Wolverhampton a few weeks earlier. Here indeed was Gladitorial Rome with men trying to destroy other men and like it was all those years ago, all in the interest of so called sport.

I have often taken part in seminars on violence and I have always said that while playing I would never do anything that could trigger a reaction on the terraces. On that particular night in Rome there was no doubt that the behaviour of the Lazio players and their Argentinian Coach was directly responsible for what was happening on the terraces. The players and the Coach were lighting the flames of hatred and violence and no one knew what the outcome would be. Here was an orchestration of the terrible and the awful. Here was the manifestation of raw and unadorned hatred.

It was the only game in my life that I found myself thinking as I was playing, "If they want it that bad, bad enough to resort to such brutal ways of unleashing physical violence onto most of my colleagues, then they could have it."

At Molineux those few weeks earlier, I warned my fellow players not to get involved in retaliatory conduct. I had a deep sense of what the outcome might be. Some colleagues took heed, others didn't.

That night in Rome our lengthy list of serious injuries bore testimony to the wisdom of my advice. I still recall the antics of the Argentinian Coach ... there he was, on the side line, roaring his support for the existing violence and his encouragement that there should be more of the same. At half-time the Lazio spectators were behaving in an alien and sub-human manner ... had it not been for the six inch reinforced glass God only knows what might have happened ... to this day I can still the squashed faces of hatred pressed hard against that glass and the efforts of the spectators to break it down and try to get to us.

The behaviour didn't change and in the second half of the game I kept thinking ... "Does it mean that much that they really want to break our legs ... for what? A football win!" The thoughts were beyond me. It might seem strange to you but even as we played the thoughts kept coming through to me ... where does this hatred come from? Why are human beings like this?

Incidentally, the coach from Argentina was the same man in charge of the team when Lazio played Arsenal in Rome a few years later. That game you may well remember was an occasion for what seemed at the time the outbreak of World War Three.

Yes I can understand the rivalry amongst teams ... a great example of the ongoing rivalry between the old firm Glasgow Rangers and Glasgow Celtic ... the verocity of their clashes is a matter of legend. Tough matches, hard fought, highly contested ... and rightly so.

What at times is difficult for me to understand is the venom from the terraces if the Greens don't beat the Blues and vice versa.

But remember, when these games are all over, the hatred seems to disappear and time and time again the spectators who confronted each other on the terraces can live in the same street and share a pint in the same pub. Again I ask myself, where does all the hatred come from?

The first and only time I actually came across hatred in any form away from a football pitch and the baying terraces was in Birmingham during November 1974. I had been broadcasting at the time for more than four years having presented a live radio programme on Friday evenings.

The programme was on B.B.C. and that involvement began when Denis MacShane, now a Labour M.P. who represents a constituency in Rotherham (he was then the youngest producer in the history of the B.B.C.) asked me to come to the B.B.C. Local Radio had just started.

Denis was an active trade unionist, a complete upstart, a maverick and without doubt, a young Jack the Lad. He had seen me on I.T.V.'s World Cup Panel covering the 1970 finals which were played in Brazil. The panel on that occasion was Paddy Crerand, Malcom Allison, Bob McNab, Jimmy Hill and myself and we had been very successful ... it was felt that we were more watchable and interesting than the B.B.C. panel. We were more controversial and willing to go out on a limb; the B.B.C. people were more cautious and, in the view of many, a great deal less colourful. These were the reasons for the MacShane approach.

The Birmingham bombings happened the previous week-end. I was completely devastated ... here was human suffering at the extremes and it was right on my doorstep.

Fortunately for me and my handful of Irish colleagues at Wolves, we experienced no hostility from our English friends and fellow players; neither did hostility come from the good people of Wolverhampton themselves.

There was most certainly no reaction from our supporters who came from all over the country. "The Wolves" had been the giants of English football during the fifties and had attracted a cult following that has lasted until this day. Almost immediately after the horrific tragedy in Birmingham the Wolves Club Chairman, the late John Ireland (an Englishman) sent for me to come round to his house called "Homestead" in Wrottesley Road. I arrived and rang the door bell. Mrs. Ireland greeted me, as always, with open arms, embraced me, held me for a few seconds.

No words were spoken but I knew exactly how she felt and what was going on in her mind. She took me through her warm trail of passages that led to Mr. Ireland in his favourite seat in one of his domestic dens.

The man got up and greeted me with the firmest and warmest handshake that I had ever experienced up until then.

"How are you big fella?"

Mr. Ireland always called me either Big Fella or Big Man. I hardly recall the Chairman ever addressing me by the name Derek or Doog.

"Would you like a drink?" he asked. Mr. Ireland was known to like a wee drop of Scotch. I replied that I would like a cup of tea.

"Are you sure," he asked, "nothing stronger?"

"A cup of tea would be fine," I replied.

"Joyce ... make the man some tea."

Chairman John had this to say: "Joyce and I, on behalf of our family, wish to express our deepest respect and understanding to you and all of the Irish people, especially

those in Ireland. After what happened here over the weekend we now know first hand what your people have been
going through for the past five years.

If there is anything we can do to help, please ... please
don't hesitate to ask."

We continued our conversation for quite some time
before I said my good byes. It was gratifying to know that
this fine gentleman who turned out to be the best Director
and Chairman of a football club that I had ever come
across bore no grudges against the Irish, wherever they
came from.

As I was driving home to my family I couldn't get John
Ireland out of my head. I thought to myself. "Now there's
a big man in every way."

But I was lucky. All sorts of people who had an Irish
accent were forced to endure and experience a period in
England which can only be said to have come from the
darkest of dark ages.

It seemed to those across the water that everyone from
Ireland, North or South, and had an Irish accent, were
fair game to all and sundary to receive physical abuse,
intimidation, harassment and rejection in pubs and restaurants.

I have known of people who were turned away from
shops and supermarkets when all they wanted to do was
to buy food for their families.

Over the years I have come across Irish people both in
Ireland and in the U.K. who have either lived in England,
come to work there or holidayed there ... all experienced
horrendous attitudes of hatred because of the Birmingham
Bombings.

I would not have expected attitudes of ignorance and
hatred at the heart of the B.B.C. in Pebble Mill. But it was
there. On the 23rd November 1974 just after two o'clock
I arrived at the Mill to present my show. En route to Denis
MacShane's office in the radio department I passed the

television area ... so far, two minutes in from the car park, no problems.

There at the end of the corridor and approaching me were two women broadcasting colleagues. We had known each other for four years.

I gave them my usual greeting ... "Hello girls ... how are you?"

The response was cold and silent. The look on the face of one of the women was harsh, empty and chilling. That emptiness struck deeply and I knew that the events of the previous week-end were now being brought into focus.

The women then addressed me directly. The Irish, in their view, and that included me, were the scum of the earth. I rocked back on my heels not believing what I was hearing. I took it for a few seconds, like somehow you do and then replied.... "Look I am the same bloke that I was last Friday when your greetings were warm and friendly."

Then it was almost naturally into attack mode ... but not attack in the irrational angry sense, but an attack born out of adrenalin and the need to defend.

"Look don't you think that I felt the same as you when I heard the news. I was disgusted, full of revulsion. My wife cried and our hearts went out to all those young people who had been murdered and maimed."

Triumph is not a word I would use in the context of people having died in such a terrible way but the manner of those two women made me want to exclaim, to put them down, to tell them they were wrong ... to triumph over them in that situation. They were wrong ... terribly wrong and I was telling them that they were wrong ... not just me Derek Dougan, but at that moment in Pebble Mill I felt that I was speaking for all of the ordinary men, women and children from my homeland in Ireland. How could John Ireland be so right ... how could these two be so wrong.

I told the women that the people who bombed Birmingham were not the same Irish as me ... in fact, I told them the terrorists were not the same people as the millions of ordinary folk in Ireland and in England.

Good people hated what had been done in Birmingham and could not be held to blame.

Again ... stoney silence from the women.

I went on to say that I could honestly understand the feelings being expressed and why those two women were behaving towards me as they were.

Again ... stoney silence from the women.

But by this time my words must have been flashing through their minds ... eye contact was avoided, body language became awkward ... a point against hatred, I felt, had been well made.

I left them and proceeded to Denis MacShane's office. Two hours later and before I was about to go on air one of the women came into studio and approached me. She tried to offer a garbled apology.

I simply said that I could fully understand how she felt.

Over the years I have given up thinking about the evil men and women who perpetrate such inhuman acts against mankind and, in particular, what I would like to do to them if I could.

Evil people who single out innocence and vulnerability to press gang them into being human bombs, van and car bombs, hostages and the victims of murder.

What people, what evil.

There is no cause or issue on this planet that is worthy of such unworthy action. I will say again and again that the people who carry out such wilful and obscene behaviour are not and never will be the same Irish as me.

Again I ask, where does all the hatred come from.

And that reminds me of Belfast.

One day in Sandy Row I asked a wee man why he hated people from the Falls road ...

"Because I do," was his reply.

I repeated the question ... his reply was the same.

I asked him again ... "I told you ... are you stupid, I just do."

You will not be surprised to learn that when, at another time, I put the same questions to a man from the Falls, his responses were exactly the same.

Yet the irony of the two men is that if you were to take them out of Belfast and put them into any street in England, Scotland or Wales, living next door to each other, I'll bet you that within a week they would be socialising together.

I know. I've seen it.

Again I ask, where does the hatred come from?

Here's a story for you ... Have you seen the film, "Missippi Burning" starring Gene Hackman and William Dafoe?

The plot is about the troubles in America's deep south. In a bedroom scene in a hotel, Dafoe asks Hackman, "Where does all the hatred come from?"

Hackman tells the story of his deep south father and a mule that a black man, a neighbour, owned. If you haven't seen the film it is well worth watching for it will give you a unique insight into deliberate prejudice, bias and hatred.

No so long ago a colleague of mine was repairing a wee woman's suite of furniture up the Shankill road. The woman knew the man well and that he was of a different religious persuasion. He was made more than welcome in her home. There were, of course, endless cups of tea and one day the woman said to him. "Son, do you know the difference between you and me?"

He looked at her in all innocence and said.

"No Missus."

The woman replied.

"The difference between you and me son is our different slogans."

Think about it ... her house ... the pictures of her loyalty, the Queen on one wall and Winston Churchill on the other. For her it was Church on Sunday, for him, Chapel and Mass.

His house ... the Sacred Heart Lamp, a Papal Blessing and a picture of the Pope. How true.

As the old Yorkshire saying goes. "There's nowt so queer as folk!"

I played in the Northern Ireland International team for fifteen years from 1958 to 1973. The team and squad was always mixed.

Most people know I am a Protestant. My religion never was an issue that burned a chasm of division in my heart and brain ... Pat Jennings came from Newry and had he been a Zen Buddhist he in his time would have still been the greatest goalkeeper I have ever played with or against. Remember I played with Gordan Banks at Leicester for two years ... Liam O'Kane when he defended for Northern Ireland and Nottingham Forest was never shackled by the prayer mat of his devotionalism. Young Martin O'Neill, midfield and going forward for Brian Clough's Forest gave no indication that he was a Catholic or in any way different to his colleagues of another persuasion. Religion just did not feature in their public lives and it certainly didn't in the life of The Doog.

A man talked the other day about his fears for the future; he had just visited a Hospice and had come to terms with the fact that he would die sooner than most— he had six months left and it was now that he faced very important decisions and judgements ... perhaps the most important in his entire life.

He knew, like the philosophers and the Ancients of the classical world, that the boat to cross the Stikks was and would always be bereft of religious labelling. There would be no notice, "Catholics queue here ... Protestants Queue There ... Jews Here...."

There would be, if indeed there would be anything, the great mass of mankind moving on to what was to come next. . . .

Another kind of life, a Heaven? a Hell? or maybe, just maybe, nothing at all.

And if it was too be the latter, what would be so terrible . . . the man from the Hospice, and you and me, would simply remain part, an intimate part, of the spinning globe that we call our world, our home at our remote corner of the Universe. If it was to be the former then the great God or Gods of our lives and our next world would ask not, "are you a Protestant, are you a Catholic, are you a Jew?"

They would ask instead, indeed they would ask, "how did you deal with your Catholic, your Protestant, or your Muslim neighbours."

These are the things of supreme importance and central to the beating of the heart of man.

Footnote:

I say again. "Where does the hatred come from?" I believe that we have lived in a state of apartheid since 1921: a state of religious, sporting, and cultural apartheid. When I was growing up I never knew of the word "Ghetto" . . . I had never heard of the word ghetto, enclave, two different cultures, two different backgrounds, the religious divide, the two sides . . . you know what I mean.

At Mersey Street School there was no teaching about the past and the past for me would have been the years from 1921 to 1951. You do not ask questions and you are told nothing of where you came from and how we emerged as a people. Most times parents and relatives really are, and it's a terrible word to use, "ignorant" of the past and, consequently, of the present.

So how then do you get to know about yourself, your family, your family tree . . . and if you haven't got it in the case of your own parental family, how can you ever hope to find out about the people who share with you religion and culture. You don't ... It's that simple, you don't.

Josie my mother always regarded education as being important and when I went to Belfast Technical High School—and that was another experience for, for the first time ever, I had Catholics with me in class—Josie wanted me to stay there longer.

But even at that College, I still heard nothing about the past and about the two communities who share the bit of land we call Northern Ireland, the North of Ireland, Ulster, the Six Counties ... call it what you will. My isolation continued.

Again I ask, where does all the hatred come from ... the question is so serious and relevant that I sought the comfort and reaction of a very good friend and one whom I respect greatly ... in the Ulster way of saying these things, he's of a different persuasion to me.

"Patsy, here does all the hatred come from ... do you hate me?"

He responded with that devilish look he kept for occasions of such questioning ... for he had his own feelings about it too.

He smiled and sat silent for a few seconds that seemed like a long time. Patsy went on to give me the most profound responses I have ever come across.

He stretched back on the chair. "You're certainly not born with it. You don't have it when you're a toddler and escape from your Ma to the street, for maybe the first time ... experiencing mixing with other children ... when you go to school and again experience another new environment. You don't have it in those first innocent days.

"School ... that's the moment," said Patsy, "that's the time when you're made to feel bad, best or better ... at times even abused. When the language of the school yard establishes difference and children seek out the different, there exists in that melting pot the hotbed for the seeds of embryonic resentment that can and often does lead on to hatred."

Patsy said that as he got older he was increasingly disillusioned over many cases and issues. He was aware of vested interest, manipulators, notions of divide and conquer … men and women who would destroy the innocence of the early days of living and by stealth and determination and deviousness, they would enlist the young in their crusade for division. It would make them strong.

"A community together repels hatred. When people respect each other there is no place for hatred. When people play together, there is no place for hatred. When people pray together there is no room for hatred. When people go on holidays, from school, at the same time of year, they meet, and there is no room for hatred."

Patsy was by now almost incandescent with the passion of his beliefs and it was sadly the passion of the man, who in his own words, was growing older and not in a position to bring about change.

So, maybe hatred comes out of an irrational sense of fear of neighbour, what neighbour will do onto neighbour, the inability to trust fellowship and good will.

Maybe it's a tribal thing with people, from the earliest days of their nature, spotting difference and acting against it.

Maybe, just maybe, it's about ignorance and no one being taught the beauty of difference and the possibilities of great learning from other experiences.

Maybe we in Ulster have it too easy and simply have to find ways of making ourselves unhappy. Maybe hatred of neighbour and community has its first walking steps on the day or the night that friend hits friend in a street fight, or man hits woman in the caveland of their home.

The ability to hurt deeply, to kill, has, I suspect, its origins in the most simple of acts.

When Patsy had finished I thought how little difference between two men, one of whom came from a wee house at the bottom of the Falls Road ... the other from another wee house, just off the Newtownards road.

Maybe, just maybe, we're not as different as we're told we are.

Maisie and The Duke you have taught him well.

Come on think of it ... the prize for trust is great. All that is needed is for all people, Politicians, Civil Servants, Religious Leaders, Teachers and the ordinary down-to-earth people of the land, to work together on the hearts and the minds of the community over the twenty five years that lies ahead. Trust brings peace and I kid you not, the good Ulster people deserve it.

16

"Man's Inhumanity to Man"

So we go to war here in Northern Ireland because of memories and history. There is, by and large, no constant genocide on the streets, no constant murder because of a man's religion, no constant murder to retain our Ulster identity and, now especially hovering on the edge of an I.R.A. ceasefire, no constant murder in support of the political ideal of a United Ireland. Yes we have had our headline making moments of terribleness but even at the worst times of the last quarter century of "The Troubles" more people were being killed on the roads of Northern Ireland than as a result of terrorism.

So, although awful, there was always an upper limit to the degree of our suffering, a limit that ensured that we were never quite as badly off as the starving millions of Africa, the victims of war in the middle east, those who were wiped out in the napalm rain from the skies above Vietnam and, indeed, more people were dying annually as a result of murder on the streets and in the homes of New York.

The last thirty years of the twentieth century has been a cruel time for planet earth, an exemplification of the adage, "Man's Inhumanity to Man". I watched some film a few months ago of the suicide bomb attack on the American Embassy in Beirut. It was footage that had never been shown on television but was the work of professional news gathers, who quite simply in a quiet moment, decided to

put music down over the pictures. What devastating
imagery ... powerful. Soldiers trapped beneath earth and
concrete and iron. Soldiers holding onto the hands of
trapped and dying colleagues ... simple contact, human
assurance and conform, and all the time over the pictures,
the melodic constancy of the musical voice over.

Powerful staff indeed and it took me, every so briefly,
into the Cenotaph Square at Enniskillen, other hands being
held, the same comfort given and human beings dying.
I'll take to the grave with me the memory of the late
Gordon Wilson holding the hand of his dying daughter
Marie.

Here I was a spectator at a quite spectacle of human
compassion and forgiveness. I remain astounded at what
that simple man was able to achieve and to give to others
in the middle of the storm of his great personal suffering.
Gordon Wilson, a man of peace, leading the way through
a jungle of Ulster trouble.

Man's inhumanity is well documented but I have always
felt that beneath the crude external crust of Ulster and
Irish cruelty, there is a warmth and a heart of goodness.
Ulster people you known have given more money to the
charities of the developing world than anyone else in
Ireland. From the unemployed of Derry went millions of
pounds to the Concern, Oxfam and Trochaire campaigns
in Africa and India.

The Irish, the Roman Catholic Irish, always had their
"Black Babies" to support and did so generation after
generation ... a throwback to personal famine just one
hundred and fifty years ago ... perhaps, perhaps.

The Irish Protestants, well their vehicle for help was
Christian Aid and Tear Fund but, always, like in the
Catholic community, the goodness, the kind heart and the
giving were there.

There's a wee Derryman who has built much in that city
from the ruins of despair and when he and his neighbours

got Derry up and running, as they did, they turned their eyes to Africa.

The story is told by a Newryman who worked there. Here follows the story of the Derryman and the Minister for the Interior.

The Derryman was in an African field one day building a wall. He was surrounded by and being helped by a number of black people. Some in the group had had families die of starvation in the weeks before. What little building was happening was taking place against a background of deep personal tragedy. They were working hard when one day the black, pin-striped, Mercedes borne Minister for the Interior arrived to observe their labours. He alighted and took some twenty steps across the mud to greet and congratulate the by now sweating Derryman and his band of fellow workers.

"My people are so grateful that you are here with us. Are you happy being here with us. Is there anything you need?" enquired the Minister for the Interior.

"Well," says the Derryman, "I'm building a wall here but I see a lot of hunger and suffering all around. You could start to do something to solve the problem. Feed the hungry."

"Easier said than done, we have so many demands on meagre resources but we do our best."

"Your best is hardly good enough for I have seen the extent of the suffering and there's nothing more anyone else can do. It's really down to your government to act."

"It's always the case," said the Minister for the Interior, "that foreigners don't quite understand ... My people endure, my people suffer, my people sacrifice, my people will overcome."

"So," said the Derryman. "You're really telling me that your people are used to suffering and that they can handle it. Is that what you're saying?"

"In a manner of speaking ..." said the Minister for

the Interior but before he could utter another word the Derryman had put down his trowel and approached the almost Regal ministerial presence.

The Derryman "drew back" (that's a good Ulsterism for the stance adopted in the moments before hitting someone) and without warning, with the side of his guttie, hit the Minister for the Interior an unmerciful kick in the balls.

"Now ya boy ya," said the Derryman, "you tell me, did you suffer with that. I'd say you did!"

And back he went to the work.

Ulster men and women have this great capacity for love and for care. There was a great example of it on the day after the mortar bomb attack on the police station in the Catholic town of Newry. Nine officers died when a series of bombs descended on the police station at Corry's Square. The mortars had been driven in their tubes on the back of a stolen truck into the car park of a nearby disused creamery. The bombs had been primed and the timers set.

Within minutes the terrorists had escaped and there was to those close by the dull thud, thud, thud of the mortar baseplates exploding sending their deadly packages high into the air.

In the yard of the police station officers were going about their normal business, many working in the corrugated iron sheds to the back of the red bricked building. Many were in the canteen having tea or coffee. The mortars exploded above their heads. There was no escape.

That night the Roman Catholic and Protestant people of Newry took to the streets in candle lit procession, singing and praying prayers of peace. The next morning a young Roman Catholic family arrived at the front desk of the Corry Square station, still open for business, and asked, "Have you a book of condolence, we're Catholics from Newry and we'd like to sign."

The people came all day and the book of the morning

had by dusk become many books with many names and messages.

There was a similar outcry on the day that twelve members of the Parachute regiment were blown to bits at Narrow Water just north of the seaside resort of Warrenpoint. The bombs had been hidden in two positions— one in the middle of a pile of straw and hay, loaded onto an agricultural lorry that had been parked in a lay by and a second bomb, a bomb to catch out the rescuers, in the gate lodge of Narrow Water Castle.

It was the day that Lord Mountbatten and his boating crew were blown up at Mullaghmore.

At Narrow Water the soldiers died.

At Mullaghmore a Lord died.

The day was the 27th August 1979.

At Warrenpoint that night Catholics and Protestants alike braved the weather and the wrath of the terrorists to come out into the square and again, they stood side by side, they sang for peace and they prayed for peace.

So what is the message coming through all of the suffering and the response to suffering. Ulster people are good people and no one can take that away from them.

They are good in their bones, in their heads and in their hearts and, I believe, they deserve better than they've been given by those who lead them.

I've told people in England and overseas, time and time again, that my people, the Ulster Irish, are the most responsible people in the entire world.

They could never understand what I meant by that proud assertion and they often pressed me further. The answer was simplicity itself but at the same time a powerful testimony to our humanity.

"Explain, explain," was the demand.

I told them and in doing so I was telling the tale of a people who were subjected to threat and who did not give in ... what I say here about one section of the Ulster

people can, so easily but in a different way, apply to
the other. We are talking here, Protestants and Roman
Catholics. These good people, a people of tradition and
music and culture were often victims in their own land, in
their own streets, even in their own homes.

Bigotry and hurt stretched out right across my entire
community. Catholics and Protestants alike know the
heavy footstep of that terrible shadow. Bigotry. Hatred,
burnings, beatings, murders....

Here in a world of green and the fundamental happiness
that exists in small communities of pride in their little
homes, some would be burned out, and a pride in making
ends meet.

Time and time again I said, what do you do or how do
you respond when someone throws water on you and calls
you names and you have to deal with it ... you walk on
to school and you survive:

When someone throws sticks at you and as they bounce
off you wave it aside, you try to protect yourself and then
you move on:

When someone throws stones at you and you try to
avoid the blow and hopefully continue with life:

When someone throws a petrol bomb through your
window and into your little two up and two down terraced
house, you, in the morning, clear up and you try get on
with living:

When someone attacks you with a baseball bat or a
hurley stick and you try to survive it and go on:

When someone kills your child to get at you and you
say, "I have got to try to forgive" and, hopefully, to go
on and search for peace ... For more than a quarter of a
century factions throughout Northern Ireland have tried
by all manner of means to plant deep seeds of hatred and
to cultivate the atmosphere for civil war, to ignite an Irish
Armageddon, but still, in spite of all of this, the atrocities,
the barbarity ... the good people of Northern Ireland have

steadfastly resisted this call to madness and to war.

Now these are the things that make the people of Ulster the most responsible people in the world.

These good people have been led by a political hierarchy and a religious hierarchy that have let them down. Politicians in some of the finest areas, in some of the finest homes but, never, in the direct firing line of Ulster's bigotry: Church leaders removed and preaching down to the masses who were throughout the time of their suffering deeply in search of leadership and spiritual guidance.

Things changed ... The twin spires of Saint Peter's on the Falls Road is now only attended on the Sunday by the few ... the numbers of church going Christians, Protestant and Roman Catholic, from working class war zones are dropping all the time.

The men who brought us to the ceasefires of the late nineties were not the constitutional politicians from the high ground but they came from within the communities of suffering. The community need spawned the men who would lead the people out of the darkness and into a new dawn of peace.

17

"Josie and Jackie"

Twenty five years ago when Clive Allison and Margaret Busby (and I'm not kidding about the names), my publishers, asked me to write my autobiography I was more than a little doubtful ... you see only three years earlier I had done just that in my book called "Attack". I didn't think I had much more to add to what had been written then but events proved me wrong.

I had thought that it was given to a footballer to write one book and, at the time of the Allison and Busby approach, I had already completed my Magnum Opus. What more was there to say.

Discussions ensued over a period of weeks. Clive came to see me in Wolverhampton and I in turn visited him London office at 6a Noel Street. Clive was an Oxford Don and it was while an undergraduate at that great educational establishment that he met Margaret who was of Caribbean origin. They were a lovely couple; two quality human beings.

Can you imagine it, here was I a guy from the Newtownards Road deep in conversation with these two personages of learning, Doyens of the world of books ... and they wanted me to write again!

What was in their heads was something which I knew not a little about, The Troubles. They had heard me speak in public and on television and radio. They knew I was a Protestant lad who had come out of a Protestant Ghetto

and, they were well aware of that basic truth in my life. I
had never met a Roman Catholic until I was ten years of
age.

The pair eventually encouraged me to think seriously
about the idea ... the thinking occurred, the book was
born, The Sash He Never Wore.

I think now of what I thought then all those years ago.
... "Why do I want to write books?" You know the truth
as well as I do ... with the exception of the few great
authors, books don't pay the rent. It's a lonely pursuit and
one which takes the writer down the road of uncertainty
and self questioning.

The nearest I can come to an answer is that I simply
wish to propagate and stimulate reaction as a result of the
words I put on paper.

Having read and reread what I written all that time
ago (and I now most certainly do know what it is like
to live in Belfast Northern Ireland and no one can level
at me the criticism of absence) I say again to myself
and keep asking the questions ... "Why am I not
filled with hate, bitterness, prejudice, bigatory, jealousy,
resentment and intolerance?"

I think about these words so much it just isn't true. The
debate continues within the soul ... why the absence of
these baser metals and importances of life and living and
through the questioning there comes, always comes, the
same answer time and time again. Josie and Jackie, but
mostly down to the former, my Ma Josie. Why was she so
special? Why did I like her so much? Here was a woman
who was of the heart and soul of East Belfast. She breathed
the air of that place that shaped her attitudes and way of
life. For Josie it was important to instil into me her own
little book of commandments:

Do you best at school and work:
Doing your best and failing isn't the end of the world;
Don't tell lies;

If you get into trouble, your Da and I want to be the first to know;

Soap and water costs you nothing—keep clean;

There's good and bad in everyone, regardless of the colour of their skin;

If you can't do a person a good turn in life forget about it;

Should a policeman (we called them Peelers) ever knock on our door and ask for Derek Dougan, I won't even ask what you've done ... I'd simply say, "there he is, take him".

Keep away from "so and so" in the street or outside the street—My God was she so right!

She doesn't know the scraps that that last one got me into for the last Commandment of Josie always ensured that I had the courage to say "No" to invitations to be involved in escapades that I knew Josie and the Peelers wouldn't like.

It's hard to believe that those commandments from that little house in 31 Avon Street, off Dee street, in East Belfast have stayed with me and still govern the way I live my life. They were also the rubrics which governed my parenting and to this very day my two sons would know the Commandments of Josie as well as their Dad.

To all the above Commandments I've added four words and I've asked my boys to try not use these words. Here they are in no order of merit:

Hate ... Promise ... Wish ... Can't.

How come that this wee woman who was hardly ever out of the Newtownards Road and only made in my memory a few journeys down to Southern Ireland, where she had the opportunity get foodstuffs a lot cheaper than she could in the north ... how come that Josie was so wise, tolerant and respectful to other human beings.

Money ... now there's a thing ... could Josie handle money, could she heck. When I think about my Ma with her housekeeper hat on with only four and a half quid a week to look after the home and feed us all ... cloth us as well. What does "us all" mean ... eight people in our house—six kids plus Mum and Dad, all together in our little two up and two down terrace house in Avon street. Josie was great and I shudder to think of what she might have achieved had she had the opportunity of a formal education. Oh Jackie for only a couple of quid more a week we could have lived up the Holywood Road or the Belmont Road ... not, mind you, that I ever resented living in the best street in Belfast. On the contrary it was the best environment that I could have possibly grown out of.

I've always stated that if we all lived up the Stormont Road and other people, the other lot all lived up the Malone Road, we would never have had the Troubles at all.

I smile more than a little when I hear the protests of some who say ... "they've had more than us ... their rights were greater than ours!" I still think about that, what total and complete nonsense.

26th June 1955 tragedy struck ... Josie died of cancer. She hadn't even reached the age of forty five. Six kids were left in our home in Avon street. Six kids, Jackie ... Josie gone.

Explain this to me ... in the last few weeks of Josie's life I couldn't bring myself to go and see her. Those, God help us, were the days before palliative medicine, no drugs to ease her demented pain ... I couldn't stand by and see it happen. Josie was in the care of the experts ... the Doctors, the Consultants, the Professors.

I was alone with my thoughts of Josie in better times, hoping and praying, I suppose, that her end would come gently. Death did not come either quickly or easily. There was pain, much pain and in the darkest of those dark days I thought time and time again why was this happening to this great lady, the author of my commandments for life and living, the lady who knew nothing of hate and everything of love. To this day not only is she constantly in my thoughts but the irony strikes home ... had Josie lived I would have been able to have given her a life that I felt sure she richly deserved. I would have wanted to have done so much ... bigger house, different area, holidays, restaurants ... I suppose they call it the good life ... but then, would Josie have wanted it? She was the Queen of our hearts and of the neighbourhood which she shared with so many great friends. All friends together with Josie at the very centre of it all.

Maybe, just maybe, Josie went to her reward at just the right time ... from within her own community and before she would be forced to be aware of and to live with the worst excesses of a quarter century of violence in Northern Ireland. If the cancer had disappeared I am convinced at times that the extent of man's inhumanity to man in Northern Ireland would have killed my Ma, Josie.

Over the years I have made many friends who are competent and qualified doctors. Some of my friends are really outstanding surgeons. None could answer the question of why Josie got her cancer. So why, out of the blue, did my mother go that way. After all, no one in my antecedents on my mothers side ... and my Dad's side as well, had ever died of cancer. So why, so suddenly, did Josie go that way and so early. The question lingers and remains unanswered.

I know that so many people are afflicted with this terrible disease in these modern times but I thank God for medical progress and the life and times of the Hospice Movement with its McMillan Nursing outreach to bring care for the dying into their very homes. The matter goes so deep that I have time and time again, whenever asked or whenever the opportunity presents itself, gone out with others, colleagues and my special friend Eddie Marcus, to

help in the business of raising funds for that great movement, especially for the Malcolm Sargent Cancer Fund for
Children. After Josie's death my Da found a Co-op Book—
that's where she took all my brothers and sisters to buy
their clothes. The Co-op even buried Josie. In the Co-Op
Book she had left more than two hundred pounds which
had accumulated from discounts over the years.

There was the puzzle ... a woman with so little but with
the wisdom to save. What an extraordinary person was
our mother Josie! To me Jackie was a brilliant man. His
world turned upside down after the death of my Mum. He
was up in the morning at half past six making ready for
the day at the Shipyard and, with Josie gone, there came
the additional responsibility of getting the kids up and
ready for school. He worked all day and came home at six
to start making the dinner ... you could tell the day of the
week by what he cooked and what we ate.

Mondays ... the leavings of the Sunday Roast, turned
into a soup and a most excellent repast; Tuesday ...
champ, with scallions (of course) and butter and milk;
Wednesday ... fish, white, and sometimes just for a change,
the red smoked variety fried in the pan; Thursday ... Irish
Stew; Friday ... a kind of mixed grill, chops, sausages,
liver and bacon; Saturday ... the Ulster Fry.

Jackie had become a Cook and a good one at that! ...
There had been not other choice for the hard man who
riveted all day in the Shipyard. Now there's a point ...
while I made it as a footballer, Jackie in the Yard was
reckoned to be the best riveter of his generation. At times
of pressure to get a job done it wasn't unusual to have an
audience gather to see how fast Jackie Dougan could fire
them rivets into the hull of the ship being built. Boy was
I proud of him!

Since I came back to live here permanently I have
obviously met a number of people and through my involvement with Co-Operation North, I have got to know a man

called Eric Cairns, a Belfast businessman, who one day said to me,

"Did you know my Da used to work your Da down in the Yard." (It's amazing over the years how many people have said to me that they worked with my Da or me in the Shipyard)

I asked what his father did there.

"I think he was a Heater Boy and a Catch Boy to your father."

This aroused my interest to get to know more about Jackie and Eric Cairns very kindly invited me to his home in Cultra.

I had tea with Eric at his home and I met Billy, the man in question.

Billy Cairns turned out to be a real quality little man.

I was really taken aback and delighted and thrilled when he told me all about Jackie and his escapades in the Shipyard during the thirties and forties, in particular he told me that James Galway's father had worked for my Da as a Heater Boy and a Catch Boy. Having just read Galway's autobiography I was amused to find out that the great Flautist didn't know where his father had worked. His father had worked most of the time and James, take it from me, it was down in the Shipyard.

When I look back Jackie gave me every encouragement to play football. So too did my grandfather Sandy and I remember in particular that he used give me criticism over not being able kick a ball too well with my right foot. Under Sandy's demanding attention I had to learn to do better and I did.

No matter what I did in the world of sport Jackie was always there for me. ... I went through a phase when I was very keen on the boxing and, on the whole, like many sportsmen, I had an eye for most ball games. My deep regret still is that when I went to Mersey Street School we never had the opportunity of learning to play Cricket and

Rugby. It's amazing that even today certain sports remain segregated, not only in this country, but also, it's fair to say, throughout the world. Sadly, some sports are even frowned upon and I regret that the G.A.A. wouldn't open its doors to all and sundry. To have had an open welcome for all could have achieved so much in the matter of healing divisions.

After Josie died it's amazing just how much of me died with her. Suddenly there was a determination to get away from Belfast. I was playing well for Distillery and there was a lot of talk about me going to this club and that one across the water. Eventually I was transferred to Portsmouth Football Club who were hovering in the lower reaches of the First Division; those were of course the days before the Premier League. I have to say, with the benefit of hindsight, I could have gone to a better placed Club in the First Division, but the town itself was great. Portsmouth, Southsea in summertime was pure and simply magic. Here I was in a town with a climate to match the South of France and it was here that I was able to come to terms with my personal grief. England was lifting me. The different experiences of life there, with the Shipyard way behind, were having an affect on me for the better. Time, as they say, can be a good healer.

When I left Northern Ireland all those years ago I never thought I would go on to play for a quarter century as a professional and achieve a great deal on and off a soccer pitch.

In "The Sash He Never Wore" I asked my colleagues in the Northern Ireland team would they come back to the old homeland ... would the Troubles keep them away. The Troubles of course been a major deterrent in stopping them from returning and to be honest I never thought that I would come home. The great surprise for me is that out of my bunch of playing colleagues at the time I'm the only one to have returned and settled in Northern Ireland.

I'm now back ten years. I have lived here permanently for five.

During this time I have made some wonderful friendships. One in particular, a couple Patsy and Eilish Hennessey. Patsy and Eilish were born and reared in Belfast.

Patsy originally came from the bottom of the Falls, 26 John Street; they are both teachers. Eilish's mother died in the prime of life and Eilish had to take on the brunt of looking after her younger brothers and sisters. She was a great help to her father John MacElhatton. When you hear about this in conversation clearly we have much, much in common.

Patsy and I are in each others company quite often and, of course, I found out that he is a great Aston Villa man! When I heard this I was able to make one of his dreams come true.

I managed to get him a ticket to see his team play Leeds in the Coca Cola Cup Final on 24th March 1996 at Wembley. We travelled down through England to my home in Wolverhampton and for the six or seven hours together in the confined space of boat and car, we had time to talk and talk plenty we did.

I was obviously fascinated to learn from him about Maisie his mother and Joe his father. The Duke, as he was affectionately known. It's incredible . . . Patsy's background and his upbringing was almost identical to my own.

As he was telling me about his family history I realised that how similar it was to my own. But he was on one side and I was on the other. His pride in place, in home and family was simply amazing. He spoke in glowing terms about his parents and what they had done for him during his life and how thrilled they were when he became the first person from the area to go to University.

When the neighbours found out about Patsy's success there was a constant calling at the house to offer good wishes and congratulations; they took pride in that as well you see. Now I reckoned I knew how his parents and his neighbours were feeling deep down. My son, Alexander, was the first in the Dougan dynasty to go to University.

The memories of Josie came back to me. I recalled the day she learned that I had been selected to play for the Northern Ireland Schoolboy International Team. I was the first ever from our district.

Her beaming pride. Her happiness. I was proud to be Josie's son. If it hadn't been for Josie I don't think I would have taken the same trouble to ensure that my own children did well at school.

The encounter with Patsy has no doubt confirmed in my mind that there is no difference between Catholics and Protestants. No difference at all. What I do believe and believe deeply, is that we must all be encouraged and given a chance.

I know only too well that if it wasn't for the few who ought to know better, those who try to divide us, we could be building bridges between human beings and one day overcoming all that keeps us apart.

I know ... I know ... I know, that all over Northern Ireland there are thousands of families like Josie and Jackie and Maisie and Joe. In that truth lies our future, the future of our children and our children's children as well.

Footnote:

Jackie came to Wolverhampton to visit and I remember asking my Dad if he would ever agree to live in a United Ireland.

He thought long and hard, paused for some considerable time and then said: "Son, if it would stop all the bombings and the shootings and the killings and the terrible destruction of life and property I would ... but I would like it to be part of the United Kingdom...."

Well there you have it, and as the Americans would say, "the sixty four thousand dollar answer" from the man from the Shipyard, the Protestant from The Newtownards Road.

Should you require a signed book by Derek Dougan please contact:

Lagan Books
Unit A 17
Valley Business Centre
67 Church Road
Newtownabbey
Co Antrim
N. Ireland
BT36 7LS

Tel: 01232 551605

or

All Seasons Publishing
12C Monaghan Street
Newry
Co Down
N. Ireland
BT35 6AA

Tel: 01693 69201